First in the World

Part of the American Council on Education Series on Community Colleges
Richard Alfred, series editor

Titles in the series:

The Community College Series

Community colleges currently enroll 6.5 million students in 1,200 institutions—one out of every two first-time students entering college and slightly less than one-half of all undergraduate students in the nation. By 2016, they are projected to enroll 7.5 million students, many of whom will be minority, lower income, and underprepared for work and further education. They are the fastest growing segment of higher education both in number of institutions and enrollment. Yet, remarkably, they are the least understood of postsecondary institutions in terms of literature and research describing their mission and role, organization and operations, and performance. This void invites quality scholarship on a segment of higher education in which interest is high and audiences are both substantial and growing. There is much in the higher education news about community colleges, but not the critical scholarship and analysis necessary to support and sustain dialogue about issues and challenges facing them.

The Community College Series is designed to produce and deliver books on current and emerging "hot topics" in community colleges, developed from a leader and managerial point of view. Our goal is to develop distinctive books on salient topics. Each book is expected to be practical and concise, provocative and engaging, and address multiple dimensions of a topic. Most books are written by a single author—a college executive who brings expert and practical understanding to a topic; an academic or researcher who has a unique slant and bank of information to bring to a topic; a policy analyst or agency official who possesses critical insights into an issue; a think tank scholar who has the capacity to identify and examine a challenge or issue that is likely to confront community colleges in the future. To ensure practicality and different viewpoints, authors are expected to solicit and present ideas from a variety of perspectives and to include examples or case studies on how institutions and leaders might deal with the topic from a strategic and operational perspective. Finally, to ensure that each book brings maximum value to the reading audience, authors are expected to present original research and employ out-of-the-box thinking in manuscript development. Each book is expected to represent the very best thought on a topic at the time of publication.

Richard Alfred
Editor
Community College Series

First in the World

Community Colleges and America's Future

J. Noah Brown

Published in Partnership with

American Council on Education™

Leadership and Advocacy

ROWMAN & LITTLEFIELD PUBLISHERS, INC.
Lanham • Boulder • New York • Toronto • Plymouth, UK

Published in Partnership with the American Council on Education

Published by Rowman & Littlefield Publishers, Inc.
A wholly owned subsidiary of The Rowman & Littlefield Publishing Group, Inc.
4501 Forbes Boulevard, Suite 200, Lanham, Maryland 20706
www.rowman.com

10 Thornbury Road, Plymouth PL6 7PP, United Kingdom

British Library Cataloguing in Publication Information Available

Library of Congress Cataloging-in-Publication Data

Brown, J. Noah.
First in the world : community colleges and America's future / J. Noah Brown.
p. cm.
Includes bibliographical references and index.
1. Community colleges—United States. I. Title.
LB2328.15.U6B75 2012
378.1'540973—dc23
2012032246

⊖™ The paper used in this publication meets the minimum requirements of American National Standard for Information Sciences Permanence of Paper for Printed Library Materials, ANSI/NISO Z39.48-1992.

Printed in the United States of America

Contents

About the Series

First in the World: Community Colleges and America's Future written by J. Noah Brown, president and CEO of the Association of Community College Trustees, is the inaugural book in a new series on community colleges sponsored by Rowman & Littlefield Publishers. Initially developed in partnership with the American Council on Education, the series is designed to develop and deliver top-quality books written from a leader and managerial point of view on "hot topics" in community colleges. Series books are intended to be provocative and engaging as well as practical and concise. To achieve this goal, they will need to be looked to and used by leaders as a resource in decision making—anything less will constitute failure. Books are written by and for leaders with insight and experience on a challenging topic or issue—a college president bringing managerial expertise to a topic; a policy analyst possessing critical insights into an issue; a think tank scholar with a deep dive capacity to surface and examine an issue beyond the visual horizon of leaders; an academic who has conducted cutting-edge research on a provocative topic. These are the people whose talent and energy make the series singularly unique in community college education.

Series topics are selected by a nine-person national advisory panel with responsibility for weighing topics for salience and identifying authors who can deliver unique perspectives. Members of the panel are:

- Richard Alfred, emeritus professor of higher education, University of Michigan
- Linda Serra Hagedorn, professor of higher education, Iowa State University
- Jim Jacobs, president, Macomb Community College
- Scott Ralls, president, North Carolina Community College System

- Susan Slesinger, executive editor, education, *American Council on Education*
- Debbie Sydow, president, Richard Bland College
- Kathryn Thirolf, doctoral candidate, University of Michigan
- Linda Thor, chancellor, Foothill–De Anza Community College District
- Cynthia Wilson, vice president, Learning and Research League of Innovation

On average, two to three books per year will be published in the series. First-year book titles include *Re-Visioning Community Colleges* by Debbie Sydow (Richard Bland College) and Richard Alfred (University of Michigan) and *Student Success: From Boardrooms to Classrooms* by Vanessa Smith Morest (Norwalk Community College). Future-year topics will focus on organizational culture and change, academic quality, disruptive innovation, and new generation leadership.

The emerging role of community colleges in the national and world order and J. Noah Brown were the first choice of topic and author. In *First in the World*, Brown jump starts the Community College Series in precisely the way we had hoped with a book that combines elements of community college history and philosophy, public policy, social and economic forces, and issues and challenges to forge a long-term view of the interwoven future of community colleges and the nation. An experienced and heavily traveled leader with deep roots on community college campuses and strong working relationships with boards of trustees and presidents and chancellors across the nation, Brown is eminently qualified to speak to the future of community colleges. He dives into the key issues challenging our colleges—accountability, governance, resources, completion, and leadership—with an understanding of community colleges and their past, present, and future in American society that is unique among thinkers and analysts. There is a derring-do quality to his work embedded in a vision of America as a world leader fueled by a high performing educational system with community colleges at the point. Being at the point is not enough, however—as part of Brown's vision, community colleges can more accurately be described as the hub or the principal driver of the nation's ability to compete and succeed on a world stage through an educated citizenry and world-class workforce. In short, community colleges and the nation are entities of mutual benefit operating on a principle of symbiosis.

Community colleges have a history, brief as is, like no other. Like all organizations, they have a life cycle that is constantly morphing and evolving—a reality acknowledged by the question: Institutional life cycle—ascending or descending? Rather than answering this question, Brown makes the case for strong leadership in a landscape that will become increasingly turbulent. It is the terrain in which we live and work in the twenty-first century, a terrain characterized by simultaneously contradictory forces of boundary-spanning technology and sociocultural polarization, scarcity and abundance, growing demand and diminishing capacity, that makes thinking, leading, and acting strategically so critical. Institutions and leaders are under intense pressure to deliver more and better results working with finite resources. Growing demands for service are accompanied by a bevy of players in governance with needs and interests requiring attention and, to a greater extent than heretofore experienced, satisfaction. Multiple-source public support, a hallmark of an earlier day, is in free fall and "privatization" is no longer a word whispered in boardrooms. When considered in tandem with the changing accountability agendas of government agencies and influential foundations and the changing interests and expectations of students and stakeholders, it is easy to put everything in the lap of leaders. And yet, if one looks earnestly at the forces challenging our colleges and balances them against the condition of leadership—growing disinterest in leadership by second-tier administrators and the dilemma of leader succession—one is struck by the drift toward mediocrity. At the very time our colleges need the very best in leaders, they may be settling for mediocrity and not doing enough about it.

A recurring theme in the pages that follow is the imperative for leadership with accountability. Urgency certainly plays a role in leading with accountability, but it is a different type of urgency. It is not an urgency borne alone by institutions attempting to grow or to acquire resources to support growth. It is an urgency shared by institutions and a nation seeking to regain economic and technological preeminence. Pursuing and achieving such a goal is not easy. As these pages suggest, community colleges will need to make major changes in governance and assessment, resource strategies, and leader preparation to achieve a level of performance that will enable them to deliver on America's promise. Brown is on target in zeroing in on steps that community colleges will need to take to lead with accountability. He identifies desirable qualities of citizen governance and how it can be improved to bring colleges to a higher level of performance. He describes strategies that colleges can use to conserve resources while simultaneously generating new resources through entrepreneurial thinking. And he boldly describes the condition of leadership in our colleges, what institutions will need to do to prepare leaders with skills to navigate the future, and where they will find them both inside and outside of higher education.

For community colleges and the next generation of leaders, be they members of governing boards or administrators, managing change will be the one constant challenge. In the end, it is what will make the biggest difference because leading with passion and courage, even in a landscape of increasing turbulence and difficulty, trumps the dangers of complacency and mediocrity. In these pages the reader will capture the essence of the world challenge facing our nation and the unique role that community colleges can play in restoring America to world leadership and prosperity. Here is an invitation to take a journey, a timely journey, at a crucial point, in the evolution of community colleges and America.

Richard L. Alfred
Series Editor
Emeritus Professor of Higher Education
University of Michigan

Foreword

Among a host of other challenges that come knocking with insistent regularity, community colleges now face what is arguably the greatest leadership challenge in their history. In its most recent CEO compensation survey, the American Association of Community Colleges (AACC) found that of sitting community college CEOs, 75 percent plan to retire within the next ten years, and 43 percent will make that transition within the next five years. Such leadership "churn" presents governing boards with the formidable task of finding increasing numbers of qualified and diverse leaders. But more daunting, they must do so at a time when economic and political stresses on community colleges have never been more acute. Trustees are faced with recruiting the best and brightest for what many consider the toughest job in higher education.

Given that context, Association of Community College Trustees (ACCT) CEO J. Noah Brown's new work, *First in the World: Community Colleges and America's Future*, could not have come at a better time. With a thorough and contemporary grasp of the major issues confronting today's community college, he provides thoughtful analysis and a compelling argument for why business as usual is a recipe for failure, leading to what he calls the "descending cycle" of community college history.

In a clear and detailed narrative that should make this book a must-read for every community college leader, Brown makes another contribution that is long overdue: analysis of the structure and importance of the two pillars of college leadership: presidents and trustees. Too often these important roles are examined independently, but community college lay citizen boards, public servants that Brown rightly asserts "make community colleges truly American institutions," must work in tandem with presidents to ensure that both policy and operations best reflect community and student needs.

In a recent commentary for the *Community College Journal*, Western Nebraska Community College trustee Thomas Perkins underscored the critical importance of the CEO/trustee partnership:

> An informed president and board of trustees is the best cumulative strength
> for the college when dealing with negative policy and legislative issues.

Perkins further noted the importance of a "common set of principles combined with integrity and a common vision." This leadership dynamic must be the bedrock for future community college success.

No one, least of all those of us who work to advance the cause of community colleges, would deny that there are continuing hard times ahead for these uniquely American institutions. Brown provides both analysis and insight into our remarkable history and the complex evolution of our mission, as well as the major forces that challenge our way forward.

In the end, strong and impassioned leadership is our most powerful asset and our best hope.

Dr. Walter G. Bumphus
President and CEO
American Association of Community Colleges

Acknowledgments

A book of this nature would not be possible without the assistance, mentorship, and unflagging support of many, many people over the years. The ideas expressed herein are the result of more than thirty years of working in the not-for-profit sector in Washington, D.C., and have been developed and honed through countless opportunities to observe and learn from those in the position to influence and effect public policy in higher education. While it would require too many pages to acknowledge everyone who has played a pivotal role, there are those who merit special recognition.

First, I must thank the board of directors of the Association of Community College Trustees (ACCT). Their leadership, support, and encouragement made this book possible by granting me time and providing the resources necessary to pursue my writing. In particular, I must express my appreciation to the ACCT chairpersons with whom I have had the privilege of working during my tenure with the association: Montez Martin; Isobel Dvorsky; Dennis Christensen; Helen Newsome; Darrell Shumway; George Little; Brenda Knight; Dr. Richard Adams; David Rutledge; Brad Young; Ken Burke; Kitty Boyle; Lynda Stanley; Dr. Arthur Anthonisen; Dr. Thomas Bennett; Dr. Peter Sercer, Sr.; and Roberto Uranga. These men and women represent the very best in community college governance, and I am forever indebted to them for their support and unfailing trust and friendship.

Special homage must be paid to Helen Newsome, Doreen Margolin, and Celia Turner, each of whom served the association's board of directors but whose lives were tragically cut short by illness. May their memories endure forever and serve to inspire and sustain us.

The entire ACCT staff deserves many thanks. Their work and dedication to the association have allowed me the privilege of leading a growing and dynamic organization. In particular, I want to acknowledge Dr. Narcisa Polonio, vice president for education, research and board leadership services, and Jee Hang Lee, director of public policy, for being a sounding board on many an occasion, and Karen Lomax, my executive assistant, for keeping the barbarians away from my office door and reminding me to write every day. And finally, I am especially indebted to David Conner, Communications and Marketing Specialist, for his invaluable editing and many editorial contributions, without which this book would not be possible.

Thanks to Dr. Richard Alfred, professor emeritus, The University of Michigan, who served both as mentor, editor, sounding board, and, in particular, for bestowing the honor of inviting me to write a book. Susan Schlesinger, American Council on Education series editor, and Patti Davis, former acquisitions editor, Rowman & Littlefield Publishers, Inc., also deserve my thanks for their editorial support, patience and understanding during the entire process. Jin Yu, assistant editor, and Karen Ackermann, assistant managing editor, both also with Rowman & Littlefield, helped prepare the manuscript for final publication and marketing, making the finished product possible.

To my parents, June and Don Brown, who instilled in me a deep love of learning, the timeless nobility of service, and importance of honesty and integrity, mere words are inadequate to express my appreciation and love.

My incredibly inspiring wife Andra deserves special tribute and homage for her unrelenting faith and love, and constant encouragement and support during the writing of this book and throughout our magical life journey together. My wonderful daughters Julia and Sophia, thank you for being so understanding and patient with me for traveling all too frequently and for missing milestones along the way. I hope you will understand and forgive.

And finally, to all the incredible men and women who serve community colleges, who in the words of Dr. Sanford Shugart, president of Valencia College in Florida, continue "demonstrating a new kind of excellence in higher education—excellence that isn't defined by exclusivity or expensiveness," we all owe a tremendous debt of gratitude.

J. Noah Brown, Washington, D.C.

Chapter One

Tomorrow's Challenges Today

If we want things to stay as they are, things will have to change. [1]

IN THE BEGINNING

On July 12, 2011, Gateway Technical College celebrated its centennial—a significant milestone for the oldest publicly funded technical college in the nation. Located on the shores of beautiful Lake Michigan in Racine, Wisconsin, Gateway was founded in 1911 by the Wisconsin legislature and has grown from the Racine Continuation School in its earliest days, to part of a vibrant statewide, sixteen-campus technical college system, which now serves more than 400,000 students each year. The Gateway Centennial afforded me an opportunity to reflect on just how far America's community colleges have come, realizing at the same time that these institutions still have miles to go, to paraphrase American poet Robert Frost.

Before the gathering of dignitaries, including the Wisconsin governor and an assortment of state and local elected officials, I had noted: "It is vitally important that policymakers at all levels understand fully the economic prowess of our community and technical colleges."[2] America's community colleges are essential to the nation's well-being, not just to our educational infrastructure, but also to our very economic fabric. This educational-economic connection is gaining more currency yet, at the same time, it is being undermined by state and local governments that are essentially "defunding" the nation's community colleges to address other mandated priorities, such as Medicare, solvency for state employee pension programs, and crumbling physical infrastructure, to name just a few.

1

A HISTORY LIKE NO OTHER

From their widely acknowledged beginnings in 1901 with the establishment of Joliet Junior College in Illinois to the nearly 1,200 institutions of today, community colleges have been vital to America's social and economic development and prosperity. In recent years, community colleges have been dubbed "Democracy's Colleges,"[3] the "Ellis Island"[4] of higher education, and "The Community's College,"[5] each signifying the important role they have played in bringing the prospect of the American Dream through education to countless millions of native-born individuals and immigrants.

For most of those 111 years, community colleges have sought to address a multiplicity of needs and demands through innovation, flexibility, and community responsiveness. The sector has grown and prospered into a system of community-centered colleges overseen by lay citizen boards—trustee boards—whose members are either elected or appointed locally or statewide. Community college trustees serve as volunteers, typically without compensation, and are drawn from the communities in which they live and work. Trustees are the "keepers of the flame," ensuring that the colleges over which they govern remain squarely focused on needs of their individual communities and the public good. They represent their communities and our very democracy. They bring multiple perspectives and experiences and join together through the mechanism of a board to advance the public good. Lay governing boards make community colleges truly American institutions.

A Mission to Serve

Today, community colleges are many things to many people. The programs and services they provide fuel our nation's national, state, and local economies, contribute to enhancing postsecondary educational attainment of the population, and serve to buttress the workforce needs of businesses and employers—both large and small.

According to the American Association of Community Colleges (AACC), community colleges enrolled 12.4 million, or 44 percent of all the undergraduates in American higher education, during fall 2008.[6] While 60 percent of students were enrolled part-time, 40 percent were enrolled on a full-time basis.[7] At the same time, the student body of community colleges is considerably more diverse than other sectors within higher education. The average age in 2007–2008 was 28, with 45 percent between 22 and 39 years of age, and 15 percent, 40 years of age or older.[8] In terms of race and ethnicity, community colleges represent a readily accessible on-ramp to higher education, serving 44 percent of all African American students, 52 percent of Hispanic students, 55 percent of Native American students, and 45 percent of Asian/Pacific Islanders.[9]

In the last couple of years, community colleges have experienced an unprecedented enrollment explosion. Specifically, enrollment trends show that "from fall 2008 to fall 2009, enrollments were up an average 11 percent nationally, and from 2007–2009 enrollments increased nearly 17 percent."[10] The rate of high school graduates who enrolled in college also reached a record in 2009, with 70.1 percent of graduates going on to college.[11] According to a survey released by the Sallie Mae Foundation in early 2012, a growing number of these graduates elected to enroll in community colleges as their first choice of institution. Part of this shift can be attributed to the most recent economic recession, when the percentage of full-time, first-time freshman students increased, due to the relative affordability of community colleges ($2,713—average annual tuition and fees) as compared with four-year public colleges and universities ($7,605).

The economic impact of the education provided by community colleges is broad and impressive. Based upon more than 500 economic impact studies conducted at community colleges by Idaho-based Economic Modeling Specialists Inc. (EMSI), community college students contributed over $34.5 billion to the nation's economic growth in 2007–2008.[12] The EMSI data also reveal the high return on investment to students and the nation as a whole relative to the public investment community colleges receive. The data indicate "students who invest time and money in a community college education receive a 15.5 percent return on investment."[13]

Community colleges award degrees, promote transfer to four-year colleges and universities, provide relevant and targeted workforce training and certification, and prepare the majority of the nation's first-responders (police, firefighters, nurses, and emergency medical personnel). Additionally, community colleges address the educational development needs of a growing proportion of high school graduates and non-native English speakers, whose educational preparation or limited English-language skills pose significant impediments to entering and succeeding in college.

Still Largely Misunderstood

Despite their growing significance and influence, community colleges are still not well understood by policymakers or the communities that provide their lifeblood through taxes, tuition reimbursement and/or formula funding, bonds, and millages. Once viewed as "junior" colleges, our community colleges are gaining increased recognition and value. In October 2010, President Barack Obama convened the first-ever White House Summit on Community Colleges, helping to skyrocket the sector to new national prominence and greater heights of public awareness.[14] Yet, despite their increased visibility, community colleges are woefully underfunded and undervalued in spite of their many contributions.[15]

The growing economic instability and accelerating societal transformation is increasingly buffeting community colleges, threatening to knock them off course and impede their ability to provide value to communities. In short, community colleges increasingly are resource-starved, while forced to confront unpleasant and difficult choices about sustaining the breadth of their mission in the face of growing pressure to scale back program offerings, or limit enrollment because of reduced capacity.

The economic and societal forces affecting community colleges have been building for a long time and are exceedingly complex and interwoven. These forces are creating major obstacles for a sector that is frequently being asked to address academic and achievement gaps in postsecondary and K–12 education. Tragically, if left unaddressed, these forces could have disastrous consequences. They threaten to erode our nation's ability to compete effectively in the world economy. Imagine if there were no community colleges—who would step in to provide the open door to postsecondary education and, with it, entry to the American Dream without regard to socioeconomic status? Or correct the academic deficiencies of high school students by providing remedial education—or developmental education as it is frequently called—to individuals in need of college-level courses, degrees, and certificates? Or serve to integrate the hundreds of thousands of new immigrants and nonnative English speakers in our increasingly diverse nation?

PURPOSE, OBJECTIVES, AUDIENCE

Two years ago, I was approached by my colleague Richard Alfred (a well-known expert on community colleges and editor of this publication series), emeritus professor of higher education at the University of Michigan, with an interesting offer. Dick told me about a new book series on the community college, and he indicated that the publisher, Rowman & Littlefield, wanted the inaugural book in the series to discuss the public policy environment confronting community colleges as they continue their evolution through the twenty-first century. What might be learned by comparing current public policies with actual institutional practice, and what suggestions or remedies might be articulated to bring public policy and practice into better alignment? Moreover, how might the nation reimagine or reinvent its priorities to ensure a more robust and secure future for community colleges, and through them, for the nation as a whole?

Purpose

As it was explained to me, the series was seeking an individual with national experience and public policy and advocacy insight—someone who had been "on the ground" working with community college leaders and elected officials on issues of national policy and legislation, someone in the unique position to look both within and outside the world of community colleges. As Dick and I discussed the thrust of the series, I became increasingly enamored of the opportunity to bring critical policy issues facing community colleges to the forefront of our national consciousness, to a potentially broader audience, while focusing on the proven potential of community colleges to assist in transforming our economy and restoring America to a position of unquestioned economic and democratic pre-eminence in the world.

With that in mind, I set forth on a two-year mission to sharpen my insights and hone my understanding of the intersection of public policy and institutional practice. As the president of the Association of Community College Trustees (ACCT), an international community college association, I had the opportunity to travel extensively during that period, talking to community college leaders, state and local policymakers, and a wide array of public policy experts and pundits—engaging virtually anyone who had something to say or who could contribute to my understanding of the community college sector and its position within higher education and society. In doing so, I learned of many similarities and differences in the changing roles of urban, suburban, rural, and even international community colleges, including especially the greater demands placed on all of these institutions within the past few years. During this same period, I witnessed explosive growth in the recognition of and appreciation for community colleges. This growth was not accidental. Candidly, it came about from a deliberate and sustained conversation with experts and professionals about the multiplicity of intersecting societal and economic needs and the growing potential of community colleges to meet those needs. The conversations about community colleges have been generally encouraging so far; what is missing, however, is the courage and imagination to address and reengineer public policy to empower community colleges to be the critical change agents needed in our economy and society.

Objective

The overriding objective of this book is to bring greater clarity of purpose to the necessary and critical conversations needed to propel community colleges forward in meeting the challenges that they and the nation face, thereby strengthening our economic and social fabric.

Specifically, I want readers to:

1. Understand the incredible depth and breadth of the needs that community colleges serve today;
2. Be able to view community colleges in the context of societal and economic forces that are continuously reshaping our national landscape;
3. Gain greater appreciation for these institutions;
4. Recognize new possibilities for strengthening and elevating community colleges to even greater levels of importance and impact; and
5. Appreciate the vast potential of community colleges to enhance, expand, and deliver on the promise of America and our democracy—in short, to fuel the reimagination of what is possible and achievable by citizens who have equal, or at least comparable, access to quality higher education.

The book makes no pretense to serve as an academic or research-based work; rather, its objective is to highlight the major public policy issues facing community colleges, suggest how the nation can reimagine community colleges and, through them, its own destiny in the world.

Audience

America has always benefited from big ideas. Community colleges represent one of the most successful and enduring big ideas in the past 111 years. My hope is that the audience for this book will encompass academicians, higher education practitioners, and association leaders, but not be limited to these individuals. Policymakers, economists, social scientists, demographers, pundits, analysts, and elected and appointed officials need to deepen their understanding of the role of community colleges and the challenges they face. Graduate students and prospective community college leaders and trustees also should read this book and engage in thoughtful and deliberate discourse about how they might guide and shape community colleges in the future.

My hope is that what is contained in these pages might prove to be the stuff of a renewed emphasis on community colleges and our historical destiny as an innovative democratic country founded on the principle of being a catalyst for good in the world. Community colleges and our nation's need to move forward are inexorably linked and mutually dependent. The citizens and leaders of this nation must reengage in a conversation about big ideas—those initiatives and goals that helped define and secure our place in the world. Community colleges were born of big ideas; they were fueled and nurtured by a collective understanding that an educated citizenry and an adherence to the principles of access and expanded opportunity were fundamental to building the nation's capacity. Not since it attained its independence has the United States of America embarked on a more important mission—promoting universal access to college.

INSTITUTIONAL LIFE CYCLE: ASCENDING OR DESCENDING?

As mentioned previously, community colleges were born in 1901 with the founding of Joliet Junior College just southwest of Chicago, Illinois. Like all social entities, community colleges have a life cycle that includes birth, growth, maturity, and the inescapable reality of measurable decline and demise. I believe that community colleges today have reached a high level of maturity, after a long period of growth and increasing acceptance. But maturity comes with challenges and limitations. What has led to growth and prosperity for the better part of a century is now threatened by economic and resource constraints, burgeoning demand and strained capacity, more students needing remediation in basic math and English, growing student diversity, fortified silos among educational sectors, demands for greater and measurable outcomes, and questions related to the value and purpose of higher education.

The first century of community colleges might be described as "ascending." The second century might be the harbinger of a descending cycle, should we needlessly fail to confront the challenges associated with growth and increased maturity. Community college leaders will need to avoid Albert Einstein's widely quoted warning about insanity—"doing the same thing over and over again and expecting different results"[16]—to avoid such a fate. To combat a descent in the life cycle, community college leaders will need to balance capacity and growth without seriously violating either, lest undesirable consequences occur. The microeconomic theory "law of diminished returns" also applies to community college capacity and output. Continuously adding programs and services to meet growing demands (enrollment costs), while not rescaling or re-evaluating current program and service effectiveness (capacity), constitutes a high-stakes game that institutions can ill-afford to sustain for any length of time. A good example of how community colleges have sought to increase programs and services by holding marginal costs low is increased dependence on part-time faculty. Because part-time faculty does not receive employment benefits through the college, colleges are able to deflate instructional costs. Hiring part-time faculty represents an economic remedy to maintaining or increasing institutional output.[17] Administrators often debate and have yet to achieve consensus on whether greater reliance on part-time faculty affects overall student success—either positively or negatively.

The Issues

Reflecting on the life cycle of community colleges, I decided to focus this book on five major issues that bring challenges and opportunities to community college leaders both today and tomorrow. I have come to believe that these issues are most crucial to the life cycle of community colleges given the extent to which they, individually and cumulatively, have the power to benefit or threaten the long-term health and vigor of community colleges. While by no means an exhaustive list, the issues on which the chapters that follow focus are:

1. Leading with Accountability;
2. Citizen Governance;
3. Resources and Scarcity;
4. Completion Matters; and
5. Leadership Imperatives.

These are five defining issues for community colleges as they struggle to maintain their level of maturity over the next one-hundred years. How effectively these issues are understood and addressed will profoundly influence the continued success of America's community colleges and the millions of individuals whose economic prospects are inseparably interwoven with our colleges. I selected these five issues carefully, informed by countless conversations I have had with community college leaders and public officials and years of economic and policy analysis, seeking greater understanding of the forces that have shaped the United States and our community colleges. I have become convinced that we cannot address these challenges without imagining the future through big ideas, the courage to confront realities, and the conviction to sustain real and measurable change. If we can do these things, community colleges will continue to enjoy a prolonged and robust period of continued good health and relevance.

LEADING WITH ACCOUNTABILITY

In the chapter that follows, I address the imperative to assume responsibility for accountability and transparency by community college boards, presidents, administrators and faculty. Since 2006, there has been a pronounced sense of urgency for greater accountability in higher education, with profound implications for community colleges. Policymakers are focusing more and more on the need to connect public policy priorities and investments to measurable results. The forces driving the renewed emphasis on accountability stem from growing concerns about institutional "mission creep"—a diminished focus on college mission—increased federal investment in student aid, international comparisons that show the United States slipping on key indicators of educational attainment, college education that is becoming out of reach financially for many, and continuing deterioration in esteem for our public and governmental institutions and leaders.

Discontinuous Education

At the same time, enrollment patterns, particularly "discontinuous education," further complicate the process of ensuring accountability. Community college leaders decry the reality that students eschew traditional or linear (sequential) academic enrollment or progression patterns, thereby confounding traditional methods to track and monitor student persistence and academic outcomes. Community college students "stop in/stop out" of college with frequency, creating enormous challenges for institutions attempting to analyze academic completion patterns. A related challenge is the phenomenon known as "swirling." Swirling occurs when students transfer readily and repeatedly among institutions, or decide to simultaneously enroll in two or more institutions. Tracking student progress is difficult if not impossible when students engage in swirling. Then there are the life challenges for many community college students. Many students work full-time, have families of their own, have limited financial resources, come from more culturally diverse backgrounds, and/or face spoken and written language barriers. In short, life gets in the way for many students seeking to complete what they start.

Inappropriate Measures

Evaluating community colleges through traditional standards based on assumptions ascribed to "traditional" higher education—that is, the average four-year college or university—regarding enrollment patterns poses significant risks for community colleges, both because of the paucity of data and benchmarks that stack up against students' stopping in/stopping out or swirling. Historically, community college leaders have too often relied upon anecdotal information regarding the "success" of colleges when student tracking and longitudinal measures are rendered irrelevant by nonlinear enrollment patterns and behaviors. The matrices used by the federal government, the Integrated Postsecondary Education Data System (IPEDS), for example, focus heavily on graduation and transfer rates. Such matrices are unforgiving in their distortion of the true picture of what transpires in the educational paths of many community college students. States often key their own matrices to those used by the federal government, so the gap between what community colleges do and how they are judged also grows exponentially at the state level, fueling the perception of failure. Community college boards and presidents are at a disadvantage because they historically have not been engaged in federal or state policymaking when it comes to codifying measures of student success, or incentivizing model programs and practices.

Leader and board resistance to applying traditional measures of success to community colleges does not stem from a lack of confidence in the quality of community college education, but rather from the knowledge that standard four-year college and university accountability measures do not take into consideration the greatly varied missions of community colleges. Many community college students pursue their educational goals through nontraditional means and pathways, and when traditional measures are used to evaluate student success and progressions, those matrices fail to capture other equally important pathways through college and on to the workplace.

Culture of Evidence

Community colleges must define and engage fully in efforts to articulate relevant benchmarks if they are to continue to function as responsive and innovative institutions in their communities, unfettered by matrices that are unrelated to mission. These include indicators of input (enrollment, student demographics, etc.), processes (tuition/fees, faculty, curricula, etc.), and output (graduation and transfer rates, certificates, credits earned, etc.). Noncredit programs, in which a majority of critical workforce and occupation-relevant preparation occurs, must be better articulated and benchmarked to appropriate outcomes. Many students take just one or two community college classes in order to hone their occupational skills, gain a job promotion, and the like, and reasonably should be considered "success stories," but are not reflected as such in composite data.

It is incumbent upon community college leaders to develop better matrices to measure against credible indicators, simplify the process of data collection and data disaggregation, and identify the most effective means of engaging community college boards and presidents in using data to leverage policy at the state and national levels. They must develop and embrace a culture of evidence. Only then will community colleges effectively persuade policymakers to move away from accountability systems that, at best, are inappropriate and, at their worst, harmful to the missions and values of community colleges. Such matrices are discussed later in the book.

CITIZEN GOVERNANCE

Chapter 3 focuses on citizen governance—a hallmark of community colleges that defines them as uniquely community-focused institutions. Trustees are drawn from the community and give of themselves in service to their communities through the work of the community colleges they govern. Effective community college governance requires individuals of differing backgrounds and experiences to put aside their "individuality" in favor of broad-based decision making that balances the needs of specific populations with the greater good of the entire community. But because community college governance shares the same genetic propensity and "immunology" as the American body politic, individual trustees sometimes fall prey to the same weaknesses or "partisanship" that impede or undermine their responsibility to the board and the college.

Disruption

Terry O'Banion, president emeritus and senior fellow, League for Innovation in the Community College, has referred to this as the phenomenon of the "rogue trustee."[18] When a single trustee becomes disruptive, the work of the entire board can be derailed. If a single individual's interests dominate the board room and force divisions that undermine the healthy functioning of a college, the results can be disastrous for college and community alike. Events of this kind dampen morale and limit board and institutional productivity.

While "rogue trustees" certainly impede the work of the community college board and ultimately administrators and faculty, they also create collateral damage to the reputation of the college within the community. It is reasonable to indicate, however, that the failure of governance is more often a result of a failure of the board. When boards fail to know and understand individual board members—their interests, aspirations, perspectives—relationships morph into confrontation and resentment among board members. The pathway to governance must be cultivated and nurtured by identifying, grooming, and educating prospective trustees about appropriate roles as board members, the need to develop a deep understanding of the role of governance, and the partnership between board and college president.

Continuous Renewal

It must be recognized that citizen governance needs to be continually renewed and nurtured, and board members must work to ensure their own perpetuity through in-service education and training and engagement with voters and appointing authorities. This is how the lifeblood of the democracy is replenished and how citizen governance is made effective. Arkansas, North Carolina, Texas, and West Virginia currently mandate some form of trustee training and orientation. Most regional accreditation standards speak to the importance of board evaluation and self-assessment. Where trustee training is not mandated, community college state associations provide trustee training, as does the Association of Community College Trustees at the national level.

Like democracy itself, community college governance requires the engagement of sectors that can nurture, inform, and sustain broad decision-making—a governance model that balances competing needs and priorities with community needs through informed and engaged decision making. In short, the electorate and appointing authorities responsible for perpetuating democratic institutions such as community colleges must also be continuously refreshed through interaction that reinforces the tenets of effective citizen governance.

RESOURCES AND SCARCITY

In chapter 4, issues of resources and scarcity are examined. The economic recession that began in 2007 pushed the country into the worst crisis since the Great Depression. The recession and mortgage crisis, which affected the largest banking institutions, led to an economic collapse in many states, thereby further exacerbating the historical decline in public support for higher education generally and community colleges specifically. As a percentage of per capita income, higher education has been capturing less and less of the wealth created over the past forty years. In the last year alone, higher education saw state funding fall by 7.6 percent, constituting the largest decline in half a century.[19] Twenty-two states reduced funding for higher education by double-digit percentages, led by Arizona (25.1 percent), Colorado (15.4 percent), Louisiana (18.5 percent), New Hampshire (41.3 percent), Oklahoma (14.5 percent), Tennessee (15 percent), Virginia (14.5 percent) and Wisconsin (20.9 percent).[20] A recent trend analysis by the Center on Budget and Policy Priorities (CBPP) paints a sobering picture for the future of state funding. Twenty-nine states project $47 billion in revenue shortfalls for the fiscal year beginning in mid-2012.[21] Further analysis shows that state governments project an increase in K–12 enrollment of 350,000 students, and 1.7 million more students enrolled in colleges and universities, while continuing to struggle with covering the costs of Medicaid and reduced employer-provided benefits and services.[22]

Demand versus Resources

As community colleges have witnessed steady erosion in traditional state and local funding streams, the demand for their programs and services has continued to increase. Community college boards and presidents have begun debating whether to wean themselves from state coffers, thereby making them "independent" colleges no longer beholden to the state or subject to regulations tied to funding. The argument is that in many cases, a state's revenue share of community college operating costs represents less than the real cost of state regulatory compliance and reporting mandates. The marked decline in property values, relatively high unemployment, demographic shifts, and an aging population demanding more services give rise to questions concerning whether state treasuries will be able to recover to a point at which community colleges might see a return to stable state funding, let alone regain a modicum of funding equitable to other state priorities.

New Model Needed

Fundamental questions regarding the adequacy of traditional funding models are being raised by community college leaders and policymakers alike. Some people question whether traditional models are sufficient to sustain community colleges into the future, or whether new models must be considered. There has been a resurgence of interest in adding performance-based funding to state appropriations and allocation formulas, and increasing demands to "incentivize" institutional improvement by focusing institutional priorities on student success and completion/transfer rates. A common refrain centers on the capability of the nation to sustain its community colleges in the twenty-first century with a resource system balanced between federal, state, and local funding as it evolved in the latter half of the twentieth century. This debate is fueling discussions focused on new partnerships, engaging new stakeholders, philanthropy, and the need for a new compact between the public and higher education.

COMPLETION MATTERS

Chapter 5 explores the renewed imperative in America to redouble efforts to increase student persistence, success, and completion. After World War II, the United States invested significant resources in higher education as part of a coherent economic and national security strategy. As a result, educational attainment surged to its highest levels. The number of community colleges also quadrupled during the same period as policymakers and community leaders responded to President Truman's 1947 National Commission on Higher Education recommendations to greatly expand the community college system in order to "democratize" higher education.

But between the Cold War era of the 1950s and the twin oil embargoes of the 1970s, the emphasis shifted, with college degrees identified less commonly with an investment in economic and national security, and more commonly as a pathway to personal higher income and social mobility. In short, the college degree became synonymous with higher lifetime earnings—the necessary admission ticket to the American Dream. Ironically, the percentage of Americans who complete college has since declined, raising serious questions about the trajectory of higher education. Conversations about access to higher education are stubbornly giving way to debates about degree completion and accountability.

Skills and Degrees

The concurrent demand for maintaining the open door while increasing student success and completion is creating a dilemma for community college leaders. Public policy and media messaging are reinforcing the notion that more Americans need at least two years of college, further exacerbating enrollment pressure and strain on community college resources as more individuals choose to enter college. Paradoxically, prioritization of the college degree has diminished other valuable occupational pathways—areas where community colleges have fought to establish legitimacy. These include vocational and technical education, career preparation, apprenticeship, and internships, all of which enable high school graduates to enter economically viable job fields and careers where skills are paramount and a college degree less so.

Relevance

Additionally, community college leaders, like their counterparts throughout higher education, are having animated conversations about the meaning and value of "completion." Academic leaders and researchers are asking serious questions about the connection between completion and the acquisition of measurable skills and competencies. Specifically, more attention is being focused on the value and relevance of student learning—a measure of output considerably beyond the notion that earning a degree or certificate or occupational certification is a proxy of ability and employability. The latter point is essential to the debate and direction of public policy surrounding public and private investment in college. Community college boards, presidents, and practitioners must address balancing student enrollment patterns, goals, and aspirations with the need to measure and assess the value of programs and credentials to assure relevance and efficiency in an era of resource scarcity.

LEADERSHIP IMPERATIVES

As the search intensifies for resources to sustain community colleges in serving the nation's needs, chapter 6 explores how community college boards are facing their most serious challenge yet: effective leadership—which if not sufficiently addressed, will undermine short- and long-term development of colleges. It is estimated that three-quarters of the men and women who currently serve as community college presidents will retire over the next decade. While a number of programs have been initiated to grow the ranks of community college leaders, the impending retirement boom suggests that community college boards will be hard-pressed to find new leaders at a time when leadership will be critical to resolving some of the most serious challenges facing community colleges in more than a generation.

Changing Environment

To compound the situation, the nature of the community college presidency has changed dramatically, bringing a new level of complexity to the challenge of recruiting and attracting new leaders. There was a time when presidents were primarily academic leaders on campus. Today, they must balance their academic leadership with the need to raise money, navigate competing demands from local constituencies, and engage in local, state, and federal advocacy. These new presidential priorities require greater time spent away from the college, thereby complicating the relationship between presidents and their governing boards.

Leadership Deficit

The nation can ill-afford a leadership deficit at a time when leadership is increasingly more critical to the future of community colleges. Community college boards will need to become more intentional about presidential recruitment and presidential succession. Boards will need to look outside of the academy for new leaders, and consider individuals without traditional academic credentials, including successful business leaders, nonprofit executives, thought-leaders, politicians, and association or trade group CEOs. A key challenge for boards selecting individuals from outside of normal academic channels will be whether faculty will accept and support such leaders. Responding to faculty concerns will include strengthening traditional leadership development pathways and institutes, and doing more to identify and prepare college administrators for presidential leadership, all of which should mitigate faculty objections.

PARADOX OF THE FUTURE

In an era of continued economic stress and global market instability, community colleges are being tasked with doing more with less, as states continue to trim their support for public colleges and universities and seek more in savings from the higher education sector. From a renewed emphasis on improving completion rates to operating transparently and being accountable with respect to student achievement, the pressure on community college boards, presidents, and administrators and faculty is evident at virtually every event and gathering that convenes the nation's community college leaders. It is the fundamental paradox of our times, at least for higher education: community colleges are positioned to do the most good but increasingly strained by diminished resources and escalating demand for programs and services.

While community college leaders display passion and dedication to steering colleges through the economic storms that rage through most of America's communities, no one can predict exactly how or when those colleges will come through the turbulence into calmer waters. The situation is made worse by the rancor and partisan divide that defines our nation's politics, some of which is made manifest through the governance system of community colleges by trustees who fail to embrace principles of effective governance.

It is troubling that at the precise moment when community colleges are most needed, funding and resources are being taken away—jeopardizing community colleges' collective ability to serve as a stabilizing force and "on-ramp" to economic opportunity for millions of Americans. I have had the privilege of working closely with community college trustees and chancellors and presidents for more than sixteen years as a policy analyst, advocate, and now as the president of an international community college association. This has sharpened my focus on issues that represent perhaps the most pervasive challenges community colleges have ever faced as they move into their second century.

WHAT FOLLOWS

This book is academic neither in construction or tone, nor is it steeped in research and analytics. Rather, what follows is a modest attempt to articulate what I have learned through countless visits to community college campuses, meetings with community college boards and presidents, and multiple forums that have brought together experts and leaders from within and outside of the community college world, including White House and congressional officials, the Departments of Education and Labor, and others.

Community colleges face many challenges in the twenty-first century. The Gateway Technical College centennial was an opportunity to reflect—to be proud of and to celebrate—just how far our colleges have come as a sector. But the community college story is far from being complete. America must renew its investment in the education of its people by returning to the big ideas that led to fifty years of increasing prosperity and economic primacy in the wake of World War II. How hard community college leaders work on being transparent, accountable, and dedicated to student success and completion will determine how the next chapters in our story will be written. We must be certain that our colleges survive the current economic storms and emerge stronger, more vibrant, and more effective than ever before. I believe that they can. All of us who have an interest in America's future must recommit ourselves to ensuring that they do.

Chapter Two

Leading with Accountability

Accountable (adj.)—Liable to being called to account; answerable [1]

TO BE ACCOUNTABLE

The notion of holding something or someone accountable likely dates back to when human beings began walking the Earth and social interactions grew more complex. As long as there have been systems or structures to govern behavior, social and cultural interactions, financial investments, moral and legal systems, the notion of accountability has been omnipresent—unceasing and unwavering. In its essence, accountability is a contract for assuring that when something was promised, something tangible was delivered.

Accountability is among the hallmarks of the community college system. Community colleges are governed by lay citizens who are publicly appointed or elected, and thus are legally and ethically stewards of the public trust and empowered to pursue the public good. The community college governance structure is embedded in and imbued with the American democratic experience. Trustees give community colleges their public legitimacy as accountable community-focused institutions, responsive to meeting the education and training needs of communities and businesses who sustain institutions, through taxation, participation in institutional programs and services, and involvement in contract programs and agreements that assist in work force development.

However, it is increasingly important that community colleges define and articulate what accountability means. Specifically:

1. Besides basic definitions of accountability, what specifically should community colleges be accountable for?
2. Is the traditional system for measuring accountability sufficient for the needs of community colleges?
3. Should community colleges be held accountable in ways that differ from the past? If so, why?
4. Are there checks and balances in community college governing board operations and administrative structures that can help "objectify" a system of accountability in contrast to relying upon subjective or anecdotal student outcomes data?

While it might be obvious that all higher education institutions should be held accountable for the resources they consume and the results they produce, society has been largely content to extol the virtues of education and the imperative of building an informed citizenry. The reason that accountability has taken on a new urgency is precisely because of the immense growth in the number of individuals enrolling in higher education at all levels. Enrollment growth has led to an exponential increase in education funding and resources, while at the same time raising new concerns about the adequacy of student performance and learning outcomes. There is a nagging sense that in spite of our best intentions, accountability has become more elusive as colleges and universities have become increasingly complex.

GAINING GREATER CURRENCY

In recent years, higher education accountability has been gaining new currency in our politics. The higher education policymaking community is focusing more attention on measuring and reporting educational outcomes, which are regularly chronicled in the higher education and trade media. Policymakers in Washington, D.C., and in and around state capitals, focus on the need to make the American higher education system accountable for the results it produces and for the resources it consumes. Greater emphasis is being placed on connecting higher education programs and services more directly with economic and labor force priorities. Accountability is also driven by concerns regarding the affordability of higher education in the wake of continuous tuition and fee increases. More learners are enrolling in institutions in part because of the barrage of information touting the link between higher education and higher earnings, as well as rapidly changing workplace and employer needs that are placing a premium on postsecondary attainment and demonstrable skills.

Demand Driven

Since the end of World War II, demand for higher education has grown exponentially. This has led to the creation of a vast and highly differentiated higher education market. The market is comprised of an array of institutions, both not-for-profit and for-profit, with a myriad of missions, governance structures, resources, and facilities. Today, there is a postsecondary education institution that satisfies practically every demand niche for education and training programs and specialized services. Case in point: during academic year 2008–2009, there were a total of 6,632 higher education institutions in the United States,[2] illustrating both the robustness of the marketplace and the strong demand for postsecondary education. In highly differentiated markets (higher education can be viewed as a market system delivering goods and services), a vast array of providers enter the marketplace, charging different prices for their products and services. For instance, in 2009, the higher education system encompassed 4,474 degree-granting institutions—37 percent public not-for-profit colleges and universities, and 63 percent private not-for-profits.[3] Additionally, there are at least another 1,600 for-profit schools according to the Association of Private Sector Colleges and Universities.

Rising Costs

The growth in the higher education marketplace also has been accompanied by an increase in the cost of attendance, considerably outpacing the Consumer Price Index (CPI). According to an August 2011 *New York Times* article, "recent data shows that tuition and fees have increased 439 percent from 1982 to 2007."[4] The need to focus more intensively on student outcomes is gaining more urgency precisely because of the growth in the number of institutions, breadth of the higher education marketplace, increasing consumer demand and expectations, and the vast public resources spent to sustain higher education and student participation through federal and state student financial aid and a host of other public and private student assistance programs and scholarships.

This point about public resources and higher education performance is significant. Once the "darling" of state government, performance-based funding for higher education reached general acceptance in the 1990s, only to be abandoned by many states a generation later. With state revenues having fallen in the wake of the most recent economic recession, performance-based funding is regaining its currency among lawmakers. In 2011 alone, six state legislatures enacted variations of performance-based funding: Arkansas, Colorado, Illinois, Mississippi, Texas, and Utah.[5] Prior to 2011, a majority of the states had mandated outcomes or performance-reporting requirements. Specifically, fourteen states had funding formulas tying their appropriations for higher education to college outcomes data; twenty-one states utilized some form of performance budgeting tying appropriation decisions to college outcomes data; and forty-seven states had some form of mandated performance data reporting on graduation rates, remediation, job placement, and the like.[6] In Tennessee, community college formula funding is tied to ten key effectiveness measures, and in Indiana, Louisiana, and Pennsylvania community-college funding is assessed by the state.

CAUTION—CURVES AHEAD

There are several considerations to keep in mind when examining the short history of accountability in colleges and universities. The following list, while certainly not exhaustive, offers cautionary tales related to the challenge of identifying and measuring higher education outcomes:

1. Too often accountability has taken on the disguise of a solution in search of a imprecisely defined problem, resulting in policies or measures totally inappropriate to mission and outcomes;
2. Accountability is "hard to define, but I know it when I see it,"[7] to paraphrase former U.S. Supreme Court Justice Potter Stewart, and yet, it must be defined in a meaningful and appropriate fashion;
3. Accountability is too readily viewed as an end in and of itself—as opposed to a means through which to achieve the desired end of validating and communicating student learning outcomes;
4. Community colleges historically have not been "at the table" when higher-education accountability was being discussed and formulated by policymaking and regulatory bodies, and so they have been expected—unrealistically and unreasonably—to conform to standards established to measure the success of four-year universities;
5. Economic and financial results are not a suitable proxy for measuring the total or cumulative impact of college on student achievement and success; and
6. Accountability often fails to capture the real nature of academic work in community colleges—namely innovative and flexible education and workforce preparation for a diverse student population, and remedial and development programs to help students overcome academic or subject matter deficits.[8]

An ever-present danger of creating an accountability system for community colleges is that too often the system itself is seen as the solution to a complex web of intertwined and complex issues that drive community college academic offerings and operations. Worse yet, the comprehensive mission pursued by community colleges, differences in the locus of governance structures, funding systems, state and local laws and regulations almost ensure that "one-size-fits-all" accountability systems do immeasurable harm, or worse, totally misconstrue or misrepresent the community college. The harshness of mismatched accountability casts a dark shadow over governing boards, leaders, and faculty, who devote themselves to the mission of the college and responsiveness to the community.

The resistance to applying traditional measures of success does not stem from a lack of confidence in the quality of community college offerings, but rather from the knowledge that standard accountability measures for four-year universities do not take into consideration the varied missions of community colleges. Many students reach or exceed their educational goals through nontraditional means, but typically only traditional measures are used to evaluate success. As mentioned in the previous chapter, the enrollment patterns of stopping in and out, swirling, and discontinuous education confound the application of accountability systems developed for more traditional student-enrollment and academic-progression patterns. More important, some community college students enter the institution with no intention of graduating with a degree or certificate, but rather to gain skills that are valued by employers or to fulfill professional career goals and requirements. These varying responsibilities of community colleges necessarily tailor each college's mission, operations, and outcomes to the needs of its community. Using standard four-year university accountability measures to gauge success more often than not paints a picture of a marginally performing institution, when in reality the institution is performing its mission *and* meeting the needs of students and the community.

A CONUNDRUM

Like all of higher education, demonstrating accountability constitutes an urgent "rule of business" for community colleges. It is taking primacy over many other issues currently faced by boards, while adding an extra layer of challenge for leaders. The call for accountability presents a clear and significant challenge for community colleges.

In the January 2010 issue of *Currents* magazine, published by the Council for the Advancement and Support of Education, I highlighted the issue in the following fashion:

> Over the past several years, momentum has been building around improving U.S. higher education outcomes and demonstrating increased accountability to the public and to policymakers. The higher education accountability move-

ment reached a critical climax in 2006, with the release of the Spellings Commission on the Future of Higher Education final report, which, among other things, called on higher education to improve outcomes and provide greater accountability to the public. Then, in January 2008, the College Board's National Commission on Community Colleges issued a report, *Winning the Skills Race and Strengthening America's Middle Class*, which garnered a great deal of attention for its findings and recommendations. Among the three major recommendations, the commission called on community college leaders to "develop new accountability measures that better assess the unique and varied missions of their institutions." The College Board Commission report crystallized a longstanding conundrum for community colleges. Namely, traditional outcome measures, and particularly those collected at the federal level through the Integrated Postsecondary Education Data System (IPEDS), inadequately capture the breadth and varied missions of community colleges. [9]

The *Currents* article goes on to describe in greater detail the notion of a "conundrum of accountability," in which policymakers gauge "success" by traditional and generally accepted higher education outcome measures. Measures, such as graduation rates, transfer rates, "time to degree," persistence, and so on, are always high on the list. Holding community colleges accountable to traditional measures is inappropriate but what is worse, they portray community colleges as failing because student graduation and transfer rates are low relative to four-year college counterparts. Too often the conversation about accountability confuses "apples with oranges"—comparing narrowly defined outcome data to institutions with dissimilar and distinct service missions and student demographics—as though higher education institutions were uniform. Community colleges face unique challenges and circumstances that demand a different accountability system—one that requires matrices more carefully tailored to their institutional nature: their governance, student characteristics, mission, and program and service offerings.

Varied Governance

Community college governance systems are organized differently throughout the states. An informal survey of state higher-education governance structures reveals that half of the states have state higher education governing or coordinating boards that oversee community colleges and other institutions within their states. In a dozen states, community colleges are governed solely by a state-wide governing or coordinating body. Twenty-three states have a community or technical college state governing board, and thirty-eight states have district or local community or technical college governing or advisory boards. Some states have both local or district boards in addition to state boards, including California, North Carolina, and Virginia, to name a few. Basic governing authorities—hiring and firing presidents, approving budgets, issuing taxing or bonding authority—vary widely among community college governing bodies, whether they are local, district-wide, or statewide. Community colleges also are accountable to regional accrediting agencies and state authorities and coordinating bodies. Not surprisingly, the guidelines and rules propagated through these entities also reflect more traditional measures, although over time, more flexibility has been incorporated in light of the growing importance of community colleges.

Varied Missions

In some states, community colleges may serve as primarily a transfer role, helping to connect student populations to four-year colleges and universities. In other states, community colleges may function as comprehensive institutions, offering an array of programs and services that enable students to pursue degree, certificate, or non-credit workforce development and training programs. For instance, in Florida, nineteen of the state's twenty-eight public community colleges now offer the baccalaureate degree in certain fields. [10] Nationwide, seventeen states permit community colleges to offer baccalaureate degrees according to the Community College Baccalaureate Association. [11] Community colleges may connect in real and tangible ways to their local high schools and middle schools through formal or informal partnerships, or provide contract-training programs with local employers. Regardless of which of these programmatic formats community colleges employ, gauging success through a narrow window of measurable outcomes grossly misrepresents the mission and governance of community colleges by failing to recognize their uniqueness and connectivity to communities.

Student Diversity

Community college students constitute a diverse population. According the American Association of Community Colleges (AACC),[12] during fall 2008, 12.4 million students were enrolled in community colleges: 7.4 million in credit-bearing courses, and 5 million in noncredit courses. Sixty percent of community college students were enrolled on a full-time basis, and 40 percent part-time. The average age was twenty-eight, and the median age twenty-three; more than one-third were twenty-one years of age or younger, and 60 percent were twenty-two years of age or older. Forty-two percent of community-college students were first-generation college students (the first in their families to attend college), 12 percent had disabilities, and 3 percent were veterans.

When broken down by gender and race/ethnicity, community college students are 58 percent female and 42 percent male, with 45 percent of color: 13 percent African American, 16 percent Hispanic, 6 percent Asian/Pacific Islander, and 1 percent Native American. As a percentage of American undergraduate students, community colleges educate large shares of minorities—55 percent of Native Americans, 45 percent of Asian/Pacific Islanders, 44 percent of African Americans, and 52 percent of Hispanics.

In addition to gender and race/ethnicity diversity, community college students also are academically diverse in their abilities and overall college preparation. For instance, the percentage of students needing remedial or developmental education in community colleges varies, but according to the 2011 edition of the *Condition of Education* released by the U.S Department of Education's National Center for Education Statistics (NCES), the figure is 42 percent. Specifically, the NCES report notes, "In 2007–08, some 42 percent of first-year undergraduate students at public two-year institutions (typically community colleges) reported having ever taken a remedial college course."[13] However, according to Christopher Mullin, program director for policy analysis with the American Association of Community Colleges, higher education analysts often refer to a figure of 60 percent as the number of students needing remediation, which comes from the 2004 edition of the *Condition of Education* released by the U.S Department of Education's National Center for Education Statistics. Specifically, the 2004 report showed that 38.9 percent of 1992 high school twelfth graders who enrolled in postsecondary education *did not* take remedial coursework by the year 2000. Thus, the inverse of 38.9 percent is 61 percent, or roughly 60 percent, which represents the number that did take a remedial course. And 10 percent of students who started at a community college in 2003–2004 did not have a high school diploma when they entered the community college.

Community college students face innumerable challenges that impede their ability to maintain academic progress. For instance, many students are economically disadvantaged. In 2010–2011, 3.4 million community college students received a Pell Grant, a needs-based grant for low-income and disadvantaged students. Many students work in addition to attending college— 84 percent, with 62 percent working more than twenty hours a week, which is a known risk factor for why students drop out of programs. To illustrate the point, 47.2 percent of students starting at a community college delayed their enrollment in 2003–2004. Thirty-seven percent of students starting at a community college in 2003–2004 were financially independent, meaning they were not listed as a "financial dependent" on a family member's federal income tax form. Almost one-quarter—24 percent—of students starting at a community college in 2003–2004 had dependents of their own to support financially. And 11.8 percent of students starting at a community college in 2003–2004 were single parents balancing child-rearing responsibilities with taking courses.

Student diversity has made the task of systematizing and collecting comparable data within and among community colleges difficult. The historical mission of enabling postsecondary access for broad segments of the population has been among the principal reasons why community colleges are judged as "failing" when it comes to student persistence and completion. Any accountability system appropriate to the reality of community-college enrollment and course-taking needs to consider these student norms, and must consequently embrace appropriate matrices.

GETTING SERIOUS ABOUT ACCOUNTABILITY

As noted earlier, the accountability systems that exist today are not tailored to the needs and comprehensive mission of community colleges. In 2009, the College Board commissioned a study of state accountability systems to ascertain measures currently used to assess community college performance. The study explored a sampling of 10 state systems and found that those states together "collect data on as many as 140 specific indicators of community college performance."[14] Specifically, the study found that the most commonly used indicators could broadly be described as "input indicators," "process indicators," and "output indicators."[15] Input indicators typically examined data related to student access—enrollment, populations served, and enrollment broken out by student demographics and characteristics. Process indicators are characterized by tuition and fees, college expenditures, faculty characteristics, and breadth of programs such as vocational, remedial, dual enrollment and on-line programming. Output indicators focus on participation rates in remedial programs, graduation and transfer rates, and/or labor force participation and wage earnings.[16] The study found that among the ten states, there was relative paucity of data on key characteristics such as student background, particularly socioeconomic status, gender, age, and immigration status. These missing elements are significant to understanding the student population currently served by community colleges.

The study also confirmed a number of the concerns long voiced by community college boards and presidents. For instance, state officials described a poor fit between state measurement needs and the federal data system, the Integrated Postsecondary Education Data System (IPEDS), because states require different data than those routinely collected by the federal government. IPEDS data are mandated and collected from every institution of higher education by the U.S. Department of Education. They are widely used by policy analysts, institutional researchers, and others to study and analyze higher education. As noted earlier, observing progress through the narrow lens of graduation and transfer rates often results in a mischaracterization of community colleges as institutions that fail to "measure up."

Appropriate Fit

What assessment measures would better fit community colleges as a means for gauging their impact on students? And how would such a matrix or set of matrices be developed? In their book, *Minding the Dream*, Gail Mellow and Cynthia Heelan suggest, among other things, that community colleges:

> Precisely assess each student's level of skills, match them to a set of pedagogical and curricular experiences, measure the student's level of education upon completion, and follow the student to the next phase where those skills are to be applied . . . and then measure again. [17]

An equally important gauge, according to the authors, would be to measure each student's educational aspirations and goals at the point of matriculation and then compare them to changes in aspirations and goals in progression through the educational experience. By tracking student goals and aspirations over time, institutional researchers can control for the reality that many students lack fundamental knowledge about college-entrance policies, course prerequisites, and degree and certificate requirements. Thus, many students are ill-equipped for success, or have completely unrealistic goals and aspirations as they enter college.

Life Gets in the Way

Most students enter with the best of intentions and plan to earn a degree or credential. But life often gets in the way—especially for community college students—knocking them off their intended trajectories. The data are sobering. According to the latest study conducted by the Center for Community College Engagement (CCCE), entering student aspirations and goals reveal that 57 percent desire to complete a certificate, 79 percent expect to earn an associate degree, and 73 percent hope to transfer to a four-year institution. [18] Unfortunately, less than half (45 percent) of all students fulfill their aspirations and goals. [19] Nonetheless, Mellow and Heelan's idea is compelling and worthy of consideration as one of many elements in the complicated relationship between student behavior and educational outcomes. The authors, who have deep experience in the community college realm, understand the realities facing community college students and the complex web of intervening factors that mitigate behaviors and decision-making patterns of students.

The fundamental question is whether an accountability system can be devised and implemented in which meaningful data flow internally to community-college administrators and faculty, while also helping external stakeholders understand the return on investment of resources they provide— resources that are critical to the long-term sustainability of community colleges. The data must precisely measure the impact of programs on student achievement and success, and be correlated to student behaviors and internal and external forces that affect educational aspirations and goals. Numbers must be disaggregated so that community-college faculty and administrators can accurately gauge the impact of programs on progress following realignment of programs and services to foster student achievement and success.

VOLUNTARY SYSTEM OF ACCOUNTABILITY

The 2008 release of the College Board's National Commission on Community Colleges report, *Winning the Skills Race and Strengthening America's Middle Class*, sounded a clarion call to community-colleges to develop accountability standards that were more germane to their comprehensive mission. Specifically, the report urged that:

> [. . .] two-year college leaders develop new accountability measures that better assess the unique and varied missions of their institutions; respond to national goals for associate and bachelor's degree production; and commit themselves again to the expectation of universal student access and success. [20]

The College Board report helped galvanize community college boards and CEOs, and led two national associations, the American Association of Community Colleges and the Association of Community College Trustees, in partnership with the College Board, to propose creating the nation's first voluntary system of accountability specifically designed for community colleges. With the support of both the Bill & Melinda Gates Foundation and Lumina Foundation for Education, the three organizations began work on the Voluntary Framework of Accountability (VFA).

The VFA, while initially slow to be accepted by community college boards and CEOs, received much-needed momentum in July 2009, when President Barack Obama announced his American Graduation Initiative, which calls for colleges and universities to increase by five million the number of Americans with a college degree by the year 2020. Other organizations soon thereafter announced initiatives echoing the president's challenge. For instance, the Bill & Melinda Gates Foundation, Lumina Foundation, and other philanthropic organizations added their own calls to action, creating initiatives to encourage community colleges to refocus on student success and completion. It became abundantly clear that without an accountability system to measure and assess student progress, community colleges would be hard-pressed to drill down to understand the impact of curricula and programmatic refinements. More importantly, without an accountability system, community colleges would be at a significant disadvantage in communicating with policymakers about the results of their efforts, and unable to counter the continual barrage of criticisms about failing to serve students effectively.

The VFA is unique because it was wholly initiated by community-college leaders and it was designed by community college researchers, presidents, trustees, and nationally recognized experts. Literally dozens of community-college leaders representing the universe of community colleges—individual colleges, state systems, governing boards, policy organizations—worked together to create a voluntary system that provides a mechanism for benchmarking improvement and progress. At the heart of the VFA's development was a commission made up of college presidents, communications professionals, accountability and institutional effectiveness experts, institutional researchers, and trustee members from a cross-section of colleges.[21] These individuals focused on issues of student persistence and outcomes; workforce, economic and community development; student learning outcomes; and communications and college engagement.[22]

More than a year was spent working to identify and define measures that form the nucleus of the VFA. A national steering committee comprised of community college trustees, presidents, institutional researchers, and organizational heads regularly reviewed the work of the commission, provided guidance and direction, and helped make decisions about the data elements that were being considered and their relevance to the task of furthering community-college accountability and transparency. The data elements that ultimately are selected and refined will assist community colleges in "telling their story" to both internal and external stakeholders. This is critically important. The challenges faced by community colleges need to be confronted and addressed through data and analysis that will guide greater student persistence and success. Moreover, the VFA provides the content and core ingredients necessary to drive a more informed discussion about community college accountability and institutional effectiveness.

As a national accountability framework developed by and for community colleges, the VFA is designed specifically to provide:

> Measures appropriate to community college missions and the students served; usable and consistent definitions to enable benchmarking and collaboration; and measures by which community colleges should be held accountable and therefore can be used to influence policy conversations with stakeholders.[23]

Built by Community Colleges

The VFA is "an accountability framework *for* community colleges, *by* community colleges, that will define appropriate measures of effectiveness based upon/relevant to community colleges' missions and students."[24] Another way to think of the VFA would be to view it as a newly emerging modern language developed by community colleges, with a vocabulary that is rich and robust and will permit each and every college to express fully in an articulated fashion its mission and services it offers to their community.

As this book was being written in early 2012, the VFA was being rolled out to community colleges across the nation. In 2011, fifty-eight colleges pilot tested the VFA and rated the measures highly useful for community colleges. In 2012, VFA leaders will work to encourage as much participation as possible from community colleges across the country, while building the VFA Data Tool to collect, display, and benchmark. The web-based interface ultimately will enable colleges to show their metrics in a uniform way—with the goal of collecting the first round of data in 2013.[25] As the VFA continues its evolution and broad application, it has been envisioned that it will encompass a framework that includes:

- Defined measures in the areas of student progress and success;
- Measures of a college's ability to meet the workforce, economic, and community development needs of its service area; and
- A framework for assessing student learning outcomes, and a data collection and display tool that enables colleges to benchmark student progress and completion data against peer colleges.[26]

Student Progress and Outcomes

While, as discussed at length above, criteria applied to measure the success of community college students must necessarily be tailored to each college's role in its specific community, three areas of focus are universal and should be implemented by all colleges not only to gauge institutional progress, but also to provide a national picture of community colleges and their unique place in the American higher education. To monitor, measure, and benchmark student progress and success, the VFA focuses on developmental (remedial) education, student progress, and student outcomes.

For developmental education, colleges should look at in-house data relative to the percentage of students who attempt their first English or mathematics developmental course. Next, colleges ought to examine the percentage of students who complete the highest level of English or mathematics developmental courses. Colleges should continue to follow those students to assess the percentage of those who successfully complete their first college-level course in English or mathematics. Finally, colleges should pay attention to the percentage of students who complete all of their developmental courses.

For student progress, colleges should examine the number of college credit hours completed by students in their first term. Reaching credit "thresholds" of 24 credit hours for part-time enrollment and 42 credit hours for full-time enrollment is important, and colleges should track the percentage of students who complete credit thresholds correlated to their enrollment status as part-time or full-time. Colleges should measure retention from one semester or term to sequential semesters and correlate retention by disaggregating student cohorts. The percentage of students who actually reach the two-year threshold should be analyzed to determine certificate or degree completion, transfer to another institution, or maintenance of enrollment in the same institution. Additionally, data on the percentage of credit hours earned at the end of two years of continuous enrollment should also be tracked and correlated.

For student outcomes, colleges should examine the percentage of students who earn an associate degree at their native institution. By comparison, colleges also should look at the percentage of students who transferred to another institution and who earned an associate degree after transferring. By the same token, the percentage of students who completed a program (e.g., certificate) below the associate level, should be assessed—both for native and transfer students. Equally important is measuring the percentage of students who transfer to another institution without a degree or other recognized postsecondary credential. Students who leave their respective institutions after having attained 30 or more credits but *no* credential, and who did *not* transfer to another institution, should also be tracked. Similarly, students who left the institution with fewer than 30 credits and no credential and did not transfer to another institution should be captured as another data point. Leaders will note the marked difference between these discrete groups of students: one group having earned the same number of credits needed for an associate's degree but for one reason or another did not fulfill an associate's degree program requirements and the other more typically not having reached this attainment level. Both of these groups are far more typical of community college students than university students and are therefore very important for community colleges to track. Lastly, colleges should track students who are still enrolled after six years as well as the current average length of time for students to a degree or certificate.

Workforce, Economic, and Community Development

A critical contribution of the VFA compared with existing assessment models is encouraging colleges to track data on workforce, economic, and community development programs. Heralded by community-college boards and presidents as critically important mission components, there continues to exist a dearth of information on the impact and contribution of such programs to local, state, and national economic workforce competitiveness. It is incumbent on colleges to track this information, which could help to highlight tangible ways in which community colleges strengthen community and state economies, as well as the national economy. Ultimately, the data could reveal gaps as well as opportunities that will affect the nation's economic stability as well as its international ranking in postsecondary education attainment.

The VFA encourages colleges to collect data on their career and technical education programs. Specifically, colleges should systematically assess outcomes data for students who pursue career and technical education programs or who earn at least 90 contact hours or more in career and technical education programs. The number of career and technical education awards, licensure exam passing rates, the number of students who complete career and technical education programs or earn 90 or more contact hours and who are employed, as well as the increase in median wage earnings for students moving through career and technical education programs should be tracked and reported. Equally important and unique to the VFA is tracking non-credit students enrolled in workforce programs, the number of state- or industry-recognized credentials earned, or the number of students who transition from non-credit to credit programs. Finally, colleges should track adult basic-education programs. The percentage of students who complete adult basic-education programs and/or earn their GED diploma should be measured, as well as the percentage of those students who enroll to obtain further education, and those who become employed as a result of participating in adult basic-education programs.

Student Learning Outcomes

While data points relating to student progress and outcomes, as well as workforce, economic, and community development, are well identified by the VFA, student-learning outcomes constitute the "next frontier" in the development and maturation of a community college-centric accountability system. Established in 2008, the mission of the National Institute for Learning Outcomes Assessment (NILOA) is to discover and disseminate mechanisms through which academic programs and institutions can productively use assessment data internally to inform and strengthen undergraduate education, and externally to communicate with policymakers, families, and other stakeholders. Community college leaders and assessment and policy experts who helped develop and shepherd the VFA focused extensively on the need for community colleges to be completely transparent with regard to measuring and reporting student-learning outcomes. As the final draft of this book was being prepared, colleges participating in the VFA were being encouraged to use the framework created by the NILOA to guide them in the development of valid community college-assessment matrix. According to the NILOA website:

NILOA assists institutions and others in discovering and adopting promising practices in the assessment of college student learning outcomes. Documenting what students learn, know and can do is of growing interest to colleges and universities, accrediting groups, higher education associations, foundations and others beyond campus, including students, their families, employers, and policymakers.[27]

MUCH MORE TO BE DONE

Much more needs to be done to identify, codify, and build a learning-outcomes assessment tool for community colleges. The challenge for those who will do this important work will be to agree on exactly what should constitute learning outcomes. This ultimately will entail community college leaders and experts coming to consensus over the core elements needed to drive a learning-outcomes assessment model the outcome of which will strengthen community colleges and make them more effective. Communicating the impact of community college instruction and credentialing programs is vital to convincing governments and the public to increase investment in community colleges as effective and economically efficient institutions capable of boosting educational attainment rates and creating a strong labor force.

Chapter Three

Citizen Governance

Trustee (noun): one to whom something is entrusted[1]

HISTORICAL PERSPECTIVES

The history of community college governance is very much steeped in the story of American democracy and values that reinforce the important role public education plays in sustaining an educated citizenry. The first community college was established in 1901 in Joliet, Illinois, by William Rainey Harper, who at the time was president of the University of Chicago. The new institution, Joliet Junior College, owes its origins to an emerging movement of the time, which sought to expand access to higher education. President Harper's "junior" college still exists today as a vibrant, dynamic community college.

The community college movement was fueled by the Morrill Act of 1862 and, later, the Smith Lever Act of 1914.[2] Community colleges received a significant boost in 1947 when President Harry S. Truman's Commission on Higher Education issued its much-anticipated report, which among other things recommended that the nation:

> [. . .] develop much more extensively than at present such opportunities as are now provided in local communities by the 2-year junior college, community institute, community college, or institute of arts and sciences.[3]

The report touted the values of expanding access to public education through community colleges and, as a result, the number of community colleges quadrupled between 1947 and today—from 330 to nearly 1,200.[4] *Higher*

Education for American Democracy, today better known as The Truman
Commission Report, served to universalize the principle of "open-door" access to postsecondary education for millions of state and community resi-
dents who otherwise would not have had the opportunity to attend college.

Governance Systems Grow

As the number and geographic penetration of community colleges expanded,
so did the governance structures necessary to ensure that their mission remained focused on community needs and that they remained true to that
mission. Today's colleges have their own identities and governing systems,
reinforcing the goals of localization and community autonomy.[5] The localization of community colleges is realized through lay governance, in which
citizens are drawn from the very same communities that constitute the governing boards of the colleges.

   In 1998, the Education Commission of the States (ECS) released a report
illustrating the complexity and variation in community college governance.
The ECS report highlights the differences in how states have organized to
govern and coordinate their community colleges. Specifically:

- Eight states utilized a state board to both *coordinate and regulate* their
  community colleges;
- Eighteen states utilized a consolidated board of their four-year and two-
  year universities and colleges to *govern* their community colleges;
- Nine states employed a coordinating board to *oversee* their local community colleges;
- Eight states had independent state boards *coordinating* their local community colleges;
- Twelve states utilized a state board to *govern* their community colleges;
  and
- Eleven states had four-year universities overseeing two-year branch campuses or institutions.[6]

The complexity in governance structures reflects the evolution of community
colleges and the values embraced by the communities and states served by
these colleges. In our democracy, there is no "right way"; rather, states are
free within the framework of the U.S. Constitution to administer to their own
affairs, including education. Community colleges are state educational institutions and legal entities, chartered, licensed, and regulated primarily within
and by the states.

Continuing Evolution

Community college governance today continues to change and evolve, and maintains a complexity that is as varied as the institutions themselves. The variations encompass states with locally appointed or elected boards that govern a single college to district-wide elected or appointed boards that govern multiple colleges to state-appointed boards responsible for all of the community colleges within a state. In a dozen states—for example, Minnesota—a single statewide board appointed by the governor oversees everything from the flagship University of Minnesota to the seven Minnesota State University campuses, as well as thirty public, two-year community and technical colleges.[7] In addition, state regulations and laws governing the composition and responsibilities of community college boards are equally complex. In spite of the complexity of governing mechanisms and structures, community college governance remains at its core an enterprise in which lay citizens avail themselves to serve without compensation.[8]

LAY CITIZENS

In 2008, the Association of Community College Trustees (ACCT)—the association for which I serve as president and CEO—embarked on its first-ever longitudinal study of the more than 6,000 trustees who govern America's community colleges. The purpose of The Citizen Trustee project was to develop "the first complete picture"[9] of community college trustees across the county. The study's initial results, released in March 2010, deepened understanding of the individuals who serve as trustees—their motivations, perspectives, allegiances, satisfaction, professional and career backgrounds, and demographic characteristics.

Diverse Backgrounds

Trustees come from a variety of backgrounds but are still predominantly white (82 percent).[10] Of the remaining 18 percent of trustees, 9 percent are African-American, 4 percent Hispanic, 2 percent Asian/Pacific Islander, and the rest American Indian, of mixed race, unknown, or other.[11] The typical trustee is fifty-five years of age or older, with almost one in five (16 percent) seventy-one years of age or older.[12] Just under 25 percent of the trustees are between the ages of forty and fifty-four, and less than 5 percent are thirty-nine years of age or younger.[13] In terms of gender, two-thirds of trustees are males and one-third are females.[14] Anecdotally, we also know certain trends in the demographics of trustees: they are skewing younger than in the past and increasingly are more diverse in terms of race and ethnicity as well as gender.

Education and Income

The majority of community college trustees are college-educated. Nearly 93 percent hold a college degree; 40 percent hold a baccalaureate degree; 32 percent a master's degree; and 21 percent a doctoral or professional degree.[15] Nearly 10 percent of the trustees graduated from associate's degree-granting institutions. In terms of income, some 57 percent of the trustees reported incomes between $50,000 and $149,000 annually, with 4 percent reporting incomes of more than $500,000 annually.[16]

Commitment to Serve

Trustees reported that they spend at least six or more hours each month volunteering in their communities in addition to the time spent serving on the community college board of trustees.[17] Trustees are politically active, with more than 99 percent registered to vote, and self-reported their political party affiliation as 44 percent Republican, 39 percent Democrat, and 16 percent independent.[18] Analysis of the current structure of community college governance in the fifty states reveals that one-third of the trustees are publicly elected; one-third are appointed locally; and one-third are appointed statewide. Professionally, trustees reported that nearly 32 percent work in business and 29 percent work in the education sector.[19] Just over 11 percent of trustees work in government in addition to holding elected or appointed positions on community college boards.[20]

Level of Satisfaction

In terms of overall satisfaction with their stewardship and service, 89 percent of trustees rated their overall board experience as either "very good" or "outstanding."[21] Forty-two percent currently are serving their first term on the board, with 26 percent reporting service on their second term, and 32 percent reporting three or more terms of board service.[22] The average term length for community college trustees was reported to be 8.3 years.[23]

Challenging Times

The issues facing community college boards are increasingly complex, perpetually changing, and more challenging than ever before. Public resources have become increasingly scarce, often stretching college programs and services to the breaking point. The reliable allocation of state and local funds is now less certain, and federal student-aid dollars are by no means guaranteed as the federal government struggles to reduce the deficit and gain control over spending. Complicating matters further, community college boards face a plethora of public policy challenges. These challenges include: growing demands that community colleges become more accountable and transparent; increased state and federal regulation and reporting requirements; renewed emphasis on student success and completion; rapidly expanding student enrollments and demographic diversification; greater connectivity to economic and workforce priorities; and pressures to maintain open access while holding down tuition and fees.

The reality is that academic and business models for community colleges are coming under greater scrutiny, and governing boards are feeling growing pressure over how best to guide the operations and priorities of the colleges they govern. And, if external pressures were not enough, boards face a whole slew of internal issues, such as rising employee healthcare and benefits costs, a looming shortfall in leadership and teaching with the "graying" of presidents and faculty, aging college physical plant and infrastructures, recurrent technology upgrades to campus finance and enrollment management systems, and rising energy and maintenance costs.

The operations and decision-making of community college boards have become more visible and more apt to be chronicled in the local newspaper or broadcast live via the local cable television channel. Board business is normally conducted in the open, allowing the community ample opportunity to observe the board's work close up. While citizen governance is a hallmark of community colleges, trustees are not normally education or policy experts. A primary responsibility of lay citizens appointed or elected to community college boards is to keep the college community-focused:

> Citizen control, one of the unique features of American higher education, means that citizens—not academics, higher education experts, or government officials—are charged with protecting institutional autonomy, educational quality, and academic freedom; with guaranteeing the perpetuity of the institutions they hold in trust; and with ensuring that higher education serves the public good.[24]

PURPOSE OF BOARDS

Community college boards set the mission and policies that plan and guide the functioning of the institution. It is their responsibility to conduct their affairs with impartiality; identify, recruit, hire, and retain (when necessary) the college president; ensure adequate leadership succession planning; assume the responsibility of setting the vision for the future; oversee finances and budget; assure accountability and assessment, community representation and input; and pursue continuous improvement and board training. The roles and responsibilities of community college trustees fundamentally are the same regardless of whether trustees serve on statewide, district, or local governing boards.

High-performing boards include individuals who are passionate community leaders, motivated to make a difference within their communities. Boards foster an environment that encourages student learning and success by setting the mission, goals, and expectations for institutional performance. Mature, functioning boards avoid direct intervention or interference in daily operations of the college; rather, they create the standards by which the president, administration, and faculty discharge their professional responsibilities around student-focused education and service goals. Effective governance requires that individuals of differing backgrounds and experiences lay aside their individual agendas in favor of broad-based decision making that balances the needs of specific populations with the greater good of the community. Because community college governance shares the same genetic material and immunology as the American body politic, boards must resist "partisanship" that impedes or complicates their responsibility to the community and the college. Allowing partisanship or single interests to impinge on the business of the board can have severe consequences for the college and the community as a whole.

Because community college boards largely are made up of lay citizens interested in representing and serving their communities, but who are not trustees by profession or training, and because terms of service stagger on an ongoing basis, community college boards rely on state associations and the Association of Community College Trustees (ACCT) to serve as important sources of information on matters of governance. State associations provide education and training services. ACCT has focused exclusively on the effective practice of citizen governance since its incorporation as a not-for-profit membership organization in 1972. Over the years, ACCT has developed a checklist for effective governance, which is often cited as fundamental to the operations of community college boards.[25] Educational resources—including publications, two annual conventions, governance leadership institutes, and interactive online training programs—help to maintain continuity in board operations and also help boards move their institutions securely into the future.

Mission

The primary responsibility of the board is to set the mission of the college and make sure that mission drives college programs and activities. Virtually every community college has a mission statement that seeks to articulate in a clear and concise fashion institutional purpose and commitment to supporting community. An example is Miami Dade College in Florida:

> The Mission of Miami Dade College is to change lives through the opportunity of education. As democracy's college, MDC provides high-quality teaching and learning experiences that are accessible and affordable to meet the needs of our diverse students and prepare them to be responsible global citizens and successful lifelong learners. The College embraces its responsibility to serve as an economic, cultural and civic beacon in our community. [26]

The MDC mission statement expresses the value its governing board places on "changing lives" by providing the opportunity to pursue postsecondary education. The mission statement goes further by concisely articulating MDC's commitment and responsibility to the Greater-Miami community. The MDC mission statement is by no means unique; one will find comparable mission statements across the nation's community colleges. The mission statement also is realized through regional accreditation—a peer-review process of ascertaining whether higher education institutions deliver on their expressed goals. It is important that boards regularly review and evaluate institutional mission to ensure community relevance and transparency of programs and services provided.

Policy Setting

Boards govern through policy and they should never micromanage. Trustees are responsible for creating policies that establish the expectations necessary to guide college operations and functions. Policy should focus on the "big picture" in which the totality of community needs are carefully balanced against constituency needs. This means that boards must regularly consult with the college president to receive information necessary to guide the development, implementation, and monitoring of board policies developed with results in mind. Most important, boards must be proactive in setting policy. They must practice visionary leadership, always with an eye toward ensuring that policy is both relevant and appropriate to mission, while anticipating the ever-changing institutional and community landscape. Board policies set the operations of the board, address issues of conflict of interest, articulate with clarity the division between board and president responsibilities, embrace board development and regular self-evaluation, and most importantly, set expectations for college programs and services, as well as an institutional culture of respect and professionalism.

High-profile events involving campus shootings, violent weather out-breaks, acts of terrorism, and student or community protests remind us how important it is that boards anticipate as much as humanly possible situations that require policies guiding campus response and emergency actions. The board is not the appropriate body to implement and respond to crisis— those responsibilities rightly fall to the president and his or her senior team. Rather, it is the board that must ensure that applicable laws and regulations are both incorporated and followed in and through institutional policy. Moreover, boards must monitor institutional responses and evaluate those responses using the yardstick of policy and expectations that boards have articulated.

Planning and Guidance

Relating to policymaking, boards must embrace and reinforce a culture of institutional planning that ensures programmatic relevancy and adequate capacity going forward. Boards guide, they do not drive, institutional operations. This distinction can easily become obscured during board dialogue. In the ideal context, boards should support planning priorities that involve "structuring conversations among internal and external constituencies to instigate a collaborative process of problem identification and issue clarification."[27] Planning involves a thorough and deliberative process by which differing alternatives and approaches are weighed, discussed, and analyzed, leading to decisions that advance institutional mission and function. Board planning activities must be transparent and embrace consensus in terms of their ultimate effect on institution and community. Planning should empower and guide decision making by presidents, result in proactive resource allocation, anticipate the future, and set realistic and measurable goals. Boards must establish the standards by which college operations are carried out. This includes an ethical framework, standards and expectations for performance, and processes by which monitoring and feedback are performed.

Once the board has developed these standards, it must delegate authority to the president and executive team to ensure that the standards are imbued through the college and its operations. Presidents, administrators, and faculty need the flexibility to exercise the appropriate decision-making based on professional expertise and judgment. They must be granted the right and supported by the board in the exercise of their responsibilities. The standards developed by the board must clearly define quality for educational programs, articulate standards for student achievement and for the ethical and fair treatment of students, guide the use of funds and asset management, and create and enforce the workplace environment and applicable rules governing employees and staff.[28]

Impartiality

Boards must behave ethically and promote a positive and open environment for student learning and maintain impartiality. They must be mindful of potential or perceived conflicts of interest. It is important that boards exercise impartiality when engaging in decision-making to avoid characterizations of individual bias or favoritism. While impartial when debating, boards should be diligent and unwavering in their expectations regarding policy implementation and monitoring. Trustees should avoid confrontation, negative or destructive behaviors, and other pitfalls that undermine their ability to remain impartial. For boards to remain cohesive and high performing, trustees must work as a team toward common goals. "Boards should have structures and rules for operating that ensure they conduct their business effectively and efficiently. Board agendas should be clear and informative and board meetings run in a business-like manner."[29]

Impartiality also demands that community college boards speak with only one voice. Individual trustees may express their opinions and views during the decision-making process, but should strive to steer clear of making promises or commitments to individual constituencies that would supersede the overall jurisdiction of the board as a single entity. In the same vein, board members should avoid public criticism of either individual members or the work of the board as a whole. As individuals, trustees should avoid making commitments on behalf of the board to constituents and they should not criticize board decisions or work against board decisions. To discharge its responsibilities, the board must:

- Integrate multiple perspectives into board decision making;
- Establish and abide by rules for conducting board business;
- Speak with one voice, and support a decision of the board once it is made; and
- Recognize that power rests with the board, not individual trustees.[30]

Board/President Relations

Each board has only one employee—the system chancellor or college president—the legally empowered chief executive officer. Boards support and depend upon the president to implement policies they set on behalf of the college and the community. The president is critically important to the success of any college, and as a rule, boards take seriously their responsibility to recruit, interview, hire, and support the president. In effectively operated institutions, the board-president relationship is a true partnership that is informed through mutual respect and support, and guided through board policy regarding ethical and professional treatment of the president. In order to ensure presidential success, boards must adhere to the following:

- Endeavor to select and retain the best (president) possible;
- Define clear parameters and expectations for performance;
- Conduct periodic evaluations; provide honest and constructive feedback;
- Act ethically in the relationship with the (president);
- Support the (president); and
- Create an environment for success.[31]

Succession Planning

Recruiting, hiring, and supporting the president, while the mainstay of the board's responsibility for a mutually beneficial partnership with the president and executive team, are by no means the entirety of the board's responsibility regarding institutional leadership. The board has a fundamental responsibility to ensure leadership continuity; the board cannot allow the college to become leaderless due to unforeseen circumstances, regardless of the nature of those circumstances. Boards need to prepare for and exercise responsibility for leadership succession within the college. The board should support practices that encourage and incent the development of future leaders from within the ranks of the faculty and administrators.

Budget and Finance

Boards are the legal fiduciary agents of their colleges. Boards must know and understand the budget and finances of the colleges they govern. While boards may delegate the details of finance and budget oversight to a finance and audit committee of the board, the entire board is responsible for the fiscal functioning and auditing of the college. This requirement has taken on renewed meaning in the wake of the Wall Street and banking crises in recent years. Auditing and accounting standards continue to change as a result, and boards must be made aware of and become fully informed of budget development and fiscal monitoring. While boards should not make day-to-day decisions regarding resources and budget, they nonetheless must ensure that all applicable state and federal requirements are met. Boards should communicate clearly their expectations and priorities relative to budgeting and the resource allocation, and support the decisions of the college president in implementing board expectations.

Accountability and Assessment

Boards are responsible for holding the president accountable for college outcomes. When boards, in conjunction with the executive team, establish goals relative to student outcomes or learning, they must expect and receive relevant reports with the appropriate data that will allow them to monitor performance. As Byron and Kay McClenney of the Community College

Leadership Program at the University of Texas so often point out, data must be disaggregated if they are to have real meaning.[32] Boards need to know what is transpiring within the margins of student learning in order to truly assess effectiveness and measure student outcomes. Likewise

> [. . .] boards must monitor adherence to their policies for programs, personnel, and fiscal and asset management. They receive periodic reports from staff and review reports by and for external agencies, such as accreditation, audit, and state and federal accountability reports. All monitoring processes culminate in the evaluation of the president as the institutional leader.[33]

Community Representation and Input

Community college boards exist to represent the common good; they serve the needs of their communities and states in which they are legally constituted and sanctioned. This requires that the board must know and understand the unique and ever-changing needs of their communities and states. They must integrate many perspectives and, often, competing priorities. Board decisions must be informed by demographic, economic, and societal trends that affect the college and the community. Trustees must find appropriate avenues within their communities and through their individual community ties and affiliations to tap into channels of information available to them. They must, in effect, become experts on their own communities and be able to harmonize multiple sources of information into an overall set of mission-directed objectives and benchmarks. To ensure relevance to the community, boards must make decisions in public and must strive to have multiple public perspectives brought into the board room. In short, boards must be visionary—they must guide their colleges into the future and honor the investments made by, and the faith placed in, the institution.

Training and Continuous Improvement

Boards, like all public entities, must nurture and sustain continuous improvement that strengthens board process as transparent, democratic, and oriented toward student success and community development. Citizen governing bodies, like our democracy, must be continually renewed and nurtured, and trustees must work to ensure the board's perpetuity through new trustee orientation, in-service training, board self-evaluation, and periodic retreats focusing on continuous improvement.

At least four states have mandated statutory requirements for trustee training. North Carolina has fifty-eight community colleges, each with a local board of trustees—eight trustees are locally elected and four appointed by the governor. North Carolina General Statutes is specific about trustee training, and permits the removal of an appointed/elected trustee for failing to attend board meetings or participate in trustee orientation and education:

§ 115D 19. Removal of trustees.
(b) A board of trustees may declare vacant the office of a member who does not attend three consecutive, scheduled meetings without justifiable excuse. A board of trustees may also declare vacant the office of a member who, without justifiable excuse, does not participate within six months of appointment in a trustee orientation and education session sponsored by the North Carolina Association of Community College Trustees. The board of trustees shall notify the appropriate appointing authority of any vacancy.[34]

Arkansas, which has twenty-two community colleges—thirteen locally governed and nine under the governance structure of state universities—also requires trustee orientation and training and continuous training thereafter:

(1) (A) To receive within one (1) year of their appointment and each year thereafter a minimum of eight (8) clock hours of instruction and training, to include higher education issues, policies, laws, and the duties and responsibilities associated with the position of board member;
(B) The members of the boards of all publicly supported institutions of higher education shall receive similar instruction and training within one (1) year of their appointment or election and each year thereafter, which shall be conducted by the individual institutions.[35]

The West Virginia legislature enacted laws in 2009 requiring periodic training and development opportunities for members of institutional governing boards, including its ten community and technical colleges.[36] Texas—with sixty-seven community colleges—has statutory requirements in both its Open Meetings Act and its Public Funds Investment Act that mandate training for all elected and appointed officials, including trustees. In 2011, the Texas Legislature also enacted requirements that trustees in their first two years in office receive training from the Texas Higher Education Coordinating Board. Illinois—with forty-eight community colleges—has no statutory trustee training requirements, but the state legislature did enact provisions that all newly elected or appointed individuals, including trustees, take an online training course that focuses on the State Open Meetings Act and the Freedom of Information Act.

Helping trustees learn about and understand trends and challenges within their states is the key to building effective community college governance. At present, there are twenty-six established state community college organizations that provide differing levels of state-based trustee training.[37] The purpose of state-based trustee training embodies the following needs:

1. To provide a unique opportunity to engage in discussion of good practices in the conduct of public academic trusteeship;
2. To provide trustees with a fuller understanding of the immediate educational, social, and economic challenges facing the state; and
3. To help connect the work of trustees to the state's educational, social, and economic challenges, particularly those that require higher education leadership.[38]

Additionally, higher education accrediting agencies encourage and support trustee orientation and training as part of their responsibility for operating effectiveness. For instance, Standard IV of the Accrediting Commission for Community and Junior Colleges of the Western Association of Schools and Colleges speaks to the importance of training as follows:

> f. The governing board has a program for board development and new member orientation. It has a mechanism for providing for continuity of board membership and staggered terms of office.[39]

Other regional accrediting agency standards support similar standards that "the board systematically develops and ensures its own effectiveness."[40] It is incumbent upon boards that they participate and understand the accrediting process and the standards by which boards should adhere relative to their own development and continuous improvement.

RISING ABOVE EVERYDAY POLITICS

Community college trustees are the "eyes and ears" of their communities. As stewards of their colleges, they serve as vital linkages to peer policymakers, businesses and employers, governmental entities, and others. Trustees must be advocates for their colleges and seek opportunities to promote their colleges publicly whenever possible. At the same time, trustees also must shield their own operations and those of the college from political interference or manipulation. Being effective advocates for a college occasionally places trustees at odds with the electorate or appointing authorities, which can create conflict and confrontation. Once elected or appointed to the board, trustees should strive to focus their first loyalty to the college and its autonomous operations. Regardless of whether trustees are elected or appointed, trustees need to understand and embrace the standards of good practice for community college boards.

ACCT, in addition to promoting and fostering effective community college governance, has for many years sought to advocate for the importance of educating appointed authorities about the importance of identifying and promoting qualified community college trustee candidates. Specifically, the ACCT guidelines reinforce:

> Those with the responsibility for appointing and/or electing trustees should focus on candidates who understand and will adhere to standards of good practice. Specifically, candidates seeking membership on a community college governing board should understand and accept that the BOARD:
>
> - Derives its authority from the community and that it must always act as an advocate on behalf of the entire community;
> - Clearly defines and articulates its role;
> - Is responsible for creating and maintaining a spirit of true cooperation and a mutually supportive relationship with its CEO;
> - Always strives to differentiate between external and internal processes in the exercise of its authority;
> - And its trustee members should engage in a regular and ongoing process of in-service training and continuous improvement;
> - And its trustee members come to each meeting prepared and ready to debate issues fully and openly;
> - And its trustee members vote their conscience and support the decision or policy made;
> - Exemplify ethical behavior and conduct that is above reproach;
> - Endeavors to remain always accountable to the community; and
> - Honestly debates the issues affecting its community and speaks with one voice once a decision or policy is made. [41]

Those involved in electing and appointing trustees must understand the critical role community college boards play in assuring relevance to community needs and the independent stewardship of public assets and resources. Trustees must model and encourage an environment that is fundamentally nonpartisan and nonpoliticized. Individuals with the demonstrated commitment and desire to discharge the public good are ideal candidates for community college boards.

Electing and appointing authorities need to understand the high stakes surrounding the necessity for and nurturing of effective governance—the need for exceptional and talented individuals to avail themselves to serve on community college boards. Those entities responsible for appointing trustees—governors, mayors, local and municipal leaders—can strengthen or weaken community colleges through the individuals they place on boards. The same is true for voters who elect trustees locally. The choices made by voters directly affect the future of community colleges, just as voters collectively determine the future of our democracy. Trustees have an obligation to help influence the selection of their peers by modeling behavior and conduct that is above reproach. The true measure of trusteeship is both creating and sustaining a legacy of effective stewardship, while assuring the perpetuity of effective governance.

Chapter Four

Resources and Scarcity

We recommend that public financing of community colleges be strengthened and that states reexamine funding guidelines for these institutions. Specifically, state funding formulas should fully acknowledge the nature of services provided to part-time students and the level of support required to serve underprepared students.[1]

RESOURCE DECLINE

The quotation that begins this chapter comes from a report issued nearly a quarter of a century ago. The United States economy has undergone pronounced change in those twenty-five years, and was severely compromised by the economic recession that began in December 2007 and lasted until June 2009—a recession described by economists, policy analysts, and media commentators as the worst economic crisis since the Great Depression. As revealed over the course of the pages that follow, the recession significantly exacerbated the decline in public support for higher education in general, and community colleges specifically. Reaching its peak in June 2009, the recession eroded public revenues, causing many states and municipalities to struggle against an increasing tide of red ink.

When I began writing this book in 2011, some forty-six states had deficits, with forty-three states having been forced to cut their expenditures for higher education. As a result, the majority of community colleges saw their funding prospects diminish as states and local governments tightened their belts and shifted short-term spending priorities. According to the Center on Budget and Policy Priorities (CBPP), a nonpartisan group based in Washington, D.C., the economic realities facing states are significant and highly troubling, particularly for community colleges. Data indicate that, when compared with the previous recession (2002–2005), state budgetary short-falls have more than doubled, reaching a high in terms of a combined deficit of $191 billion.[2] By comparison, during the previous recession, combined state deficits reached a high-water mark of $80 billion, or less than half the current level of debt held by the states.

The federal government intervened during the height of the recession with the American Recovery and Reinvestment Act of 2009, or ARRA, enacted by Congress in February 2009. In response to worsening state defi-cits, ARRA temporarily forestalled cuts in state education budgets by provid-ing an infusion of funds for education and infrastructure investments between 2009 and 2010. ARRA funds were critical in providing resources to "stabi-lize state support for education among other interventions to achieve eco-nomic recovery."[3] However, most of those funds were exhausted by late 2011, and states found themselves scrambling to make up the difference. With ARRA and other attempts to stimulate the economy, the United States government added to its own budget woes by amassing the largest public debt in the nation's history—$14.8 trillion by the close of 2011, as reported by the Office of Management and Budget.

The Congressional Budget Office issued warnings in early 2012 that ab-sent significant changes in federal policy, the federal debt could rise to nearly 100 percent of gross domestic product (GDP) by the end of the next decade. This means that the true impact of the last economic recession on community colleges might not yet have been fully realized. With federal and state governments facing structural challenges resulting from revenue shortfalls and fixed cost domestic programs, community colleges face uncertainties in funding from entities that on the one hand depend on them for economic and workforce development while, on the other, provide operational and capital resources.

SCARCITY

The impact of the economic crisis and concomitant downturn in funding for higher education and community colleges is pronounced. As noted earlier, 43 states instituted cuts to public higher education institutions by the end of 2011, while also increasing tuition and fees to bridge the growing gap in state support.[4] The CBPP report on *State Budget Cuts* highlights the states that have been forced to shift responsibilities for covering the costs of public higher education:

• **Alabama** raised tuition ranging from eight to 23 percent;

- **Arizona Board of Regents** approved tuition and fee increases between nine and 20 percent;
- **University of California** has increased its tuition by more than 32 percent since 2008;
- **Colorado** slashed state support for higher education by more than $62 million;
- **Florida's** public universities anticipated raised tuition by 15 percent for the 2010–2011 academic year;
- **Georgia** cut state funding for higher education by $151 million in FY 2011; and
- **Michigan** cut student financial aid by $135 million.[5]

These are but a few of the many examples of the downward spiral in funding that has resulted from state efforts to support state services and obligations.

While states reduced spending on higher education, including community colleges, they also reduced spending in many other areas, including trimming state payrolls by reducing their workforce, reducing state purchases of goods and services, and postponing or canceling investments in infrastructure. The combined effect of these additional cuts and reductions in state spending was to further exacerbate the fiscal situation as state unemployment claims and the multiplying effect of reduced income taxes further eroded state coffers. And as home values declined and/or mortgage foreclosures increased, state and local revenues were reduced even further.

Lifeblood

The lifeblood of community colleges has been the allocation of public funds, predominantly state and local income- and property-tax revenues, which have allowed institutions to maintain an "open-door" policy for students. Community colleges are funded in a multiplicity of ways, depending on state statutes and the evolution of postsecondary funding mechanisms for community colleges in the states. Some community colleges receive funds through formula-based appropriations reflecting enrollment trends; some have authority to issue bonds for capital projects; and others can levy local tax increases on either income or property assessment values.

On average, community colleges have received 38 percent of their revenues from state government appropriations, 17 percent from local appropriations, and 25 percent from a mix of federal, state and local grants, contributions, and other sources.[6] Students contribute on average 20 percent of community-college revenues through tuition and fees paid to the institution.[7] Regardless of the source, state and local revenues constitute slightly more than half of the public resources used to support instruction, facilities, and personnel. This is wholly consistent with the compact between community colleges and state and local governments, whose constituents benefit directly from the programs, services, and revenues generated by the institutions.

Support-Demand Mismatch

Public revenues allocated to community colleges have declined while enrollment growth in community colleges reached double-digit proportions at the peak of the recession.[8] In fact, since 1974, the percentage of state tax-based revenues flowing to higher-education institutions as a percentage of overall state expenditures declined from 7.5 percent to 4.5 percent by 2008.[9] The mismatch in funding relative to enrollment growth has had a significant effect on community colleges, which as noted above depend heavily on state and local appropriations. Community-college boards and presidents are struggling with balancing increased demands with decreased public resources. In essence, the traditional resource model that has governed community college operations is becoming increasingly strained, raising the specter of a need for change in the way community college boards and presidents approach resourcing their institutions. This is a frightening prospect for boards and presidents, who are struggling to maintain open access.

Inequality

Over the past five years, enrollment in public higher-education institutions, including community colleges, has grown significantly. Full-time equivalent enrollment, (FTE), grew by more than 15 percent between FY 2005 and FY 2010, with forty-nine states reporting enrollment gains.[10] More troubling is the inverse relationship between enrollment growth and public funding. Specifically, the decline in the percentage of wealth, as measured by per capita income, was directed to support of higher education. Between 1998 and 2008, total taxable income as percentage of per capita income grew nearly 48 percent, while the effective rate of income-tax receipts funneled to higher education grew by only five percent.[11] Higher-education institutions effectively lost ground in leveraging public funding during economic expansion and wealth creation prior to 2007.

Community-college funding is complex and the way in which funding is awarded reflects the individuality of the communities and states in which community colleges are located. Specifically:

> At the state level, community college funding issues are never considered in a vacuum. Alone among education sectors, community college funding flows from both state appropriations and federally funding workforce training programs that are often matched by states and administered through non-education-related state cabinet agencies, In approximately half of the states, some or all community colleges receive funding from local government sources.[12]

Especially troubling for boards and presidents is that while community colleges constitute roughly half of the higher-education marketplace relative to student enrollment, community colleges have not commanded the same level of state investment as four-year state colleges and universities. In other words, there exists a real and measurable imbalance between the size of the population served by community colleges and the proportion of public funding they receive. For instance, in 2007–2008, community colleges received "27 percent of the total of federal, state, and local revenues" despite serving 43 percent of all undergraduate students. [13]

The situation is made worse by the fact that community colleges have historically received less of a proportion of state tax appropriations than do public higher-education institutions generally. The situation is no better at the federal level. Despite the one-third of community-college students who receive federal student aid assistance, community colleges receive significantly less federal assistance than other sectors of higher education. [14] With funding comes respect, and community colleges consequently have not received the same level of respect for their mission as state college and university systems. But a more important question must be posed: Can the nation sustain community colleges in the twenty-first century through resource and funding models developed in the twentieth century and which are failing to keep pace?

FUNDING INDEPENDENCE

Eroding public funding has led boards and presidents to reexamine how they resource programs, as they increasingly struggle to marshal scarce dollars to meet burgeoning community and business needs. The number of community colleges that have seen their budgets weaned from state coffers, either voluntarily or involuntarily, has increased—essentially raising the prospect of moving from publicly supported institutions to independent institutions. This will change the social compact between government and community colleges and challenge the historical commitment to invest as a means for providing order to provide access to postsecondary education access for a wide array of individuals. Community-college boards, presidents, and policymakers have begun in earnest to explore fundamental questions regarding funding models and to address whether traditional models are sufficient to sustain community colleges in the future, or whether new models will need to be considered.

Commitment to Students

Community colleges traditionally have concentrated their public funds on instruction. This has been a hallmark of community colleges, and boards and presidents are quick to cite their commitment to student learning and instruction as a defining characteristic of community college education. In FY 2009, community colleges spent "44.5 percent of education and general funds on instruction as compared to 39.6 percent at private research institutions, and 36.1 percent at public research institutions."[15] Their focus on student instruction and learning sets them apart from universities, where freshman and sophomore courses are larger and where students often have less interaction with faculty.

In an era of declining public resources, community colleges must make tough choices relative to support for instructional programs, and it is not unusual for students to encounter programs that are oversubscribed. High demand programs, such as nursing, are a case in point. Community-college nursing programs represent a high-quality alternative to traditional four-year RN (registered nurse) programs. Most programs are consistently over-subscribed, because of demand for nursing programs fed by a nursing shortage, and the high cost of administering nursing programs. Dependence on local funding for many colleges, once a strength, is now an increasing liability, particularly with so many municipalities and counties grappling with fiscal strain. Pressure on community-college resources is expected to worsen and the future of funding is murky at best.

EFFECTS OF SCARCITY

Community-college boards and presidents have had to contend with periods of resource scarcity before. What is different now is the prospect of a prolonged downward spiral in public funding for the majority of community colleges. This prospect could challenge community colleges to a degree not seen before. State directors of community college systems are not optimistic about the resources that will be available to community colleges. A survey of state system directors released in 2010 paints a sobering picture.[16] Demographic trends indicate that between 2009 and 2012, more than four million more eighteen- to twenty-four-year-olds will be added to the general population—a prime age-range of college attendance. Nearly one-third of the state directors reported that colleges in their states will not have the capacity to accommodate current, much less projected, student-enrollment growth. Increasing numbers of older students, returning military veterans, growing demands for distance-education programs and services, and aging college infrastructures are placing added strain on college capacity. The much-needed and widely heralded increases to the Federal Pell Grant program—a needs-based grant for low-income students—are expected to balloon community-college enrollment over the next several years. Currently, more than one-third of community college students receive Pell Grants—the most significant resource mechanism for ensuring access to postsecondary education for low-income and disadvantaged students. Enrollment caps at state universities likely will continue as these institutions struggle to contain costs and adjust to the downturn in state funding. This will create an additional choke point for community-college students attempting to transfer to four-year colleges and universities.

Psychology of Scarcity

The psychology of scarcity can be debilitating, and corrosive for colleges attempting to maintain a culture of innovation and optimism. Scarcity tends to pit constituencies against one other as they compete for attention and funds. Community-college boards have had to face unpleasant choices about spending priorities, faculty and administrator salaries and benefits, and infrastructure needs, to name a few, as they labor to keep college doors open to a growing number of learners. And the concomitant emphasis on completion and student success has caused community-college boards and presidents to worry more about how to achieve enrollment growth while simultaneously devoting resources to student persistence and completion. Presidents are on the front line of resource scarcity as they strive to find ways to advocate for their institutions—struggling to put the "best face" on a difficult situation.

Pressure to Reform

Scarcity also brings added pressure from policymakers and state leaders to address competing priorities. An ever-present danger is reform and reorganization of higher-education systems and resources:

> States' policymakers have recommended or enacted proposals to change educational delivery models. The goals are to trim, merge, consolidate, or even eliminate various higher education functions while imposing stricter accountability measures. [17]

Such reorganization and reform efforts can extend to the governance systems of community colleges. In 2011, the Connecticut State Colleges and Universities Board of Regents for Higher Education was created to oversee the state's four regional universities, twelve community colleges and, one online college. Previously, the state's community colleges were governed by a separate state board with its own chancellor. The rationale provided at the time by Connecticut governor Dannel P. Malloy was that reorganizing the state higher-education governance system would save Connecticut taxpayers an estimated $4.3 million annually.[18]

As with governance systems, scarcity can wreak havoc on politics and political systems. A 2010 article by Thomas B. Edsall in *The New Republic* magazine described the rise of the Tea Party movement in American politics, highlighting just how the debate over public resources is not a new phenomenon, but has taken on dynamic new proportions. While skirmishes over resource allocation are the traditional fodder of politics, Edsall writes:

> [. . .] it takes place in a new context—an age of growing austerity, where this complaint will acquire an ever-sharper edge and battles over the scarce resources of the state will erupt in spectacular skirmishes.[19]

Community colleges are not immune to, or isolated from, the politics that play themselves out on a daily basis in our communities, or on the state and national stage. As discussed in chapter 2, community college trustees are empowered as decision makers though the political system—via popular election or political appointment. In an era of diminished resources, community-college trustees must grapple with the same pressures felt by their political counterparts at the local, state, and national levels. This can result in conflicts between trustees and/or presidents, which corrode the "glue of good will" that keeps boards and presidents inoculated against the debilitating effects of prolonged scarcity.

WHERE TO TURN

So where are community colleges turning to find the necessary resources in an era of growing scarcity? In their book, *Minding the Dream: The Process and Practice of the American Community College*, Gail O. Mellow and Cynthia Heelan identify alternative resource strategies that are being deployed by community colleges: grants and contracts; philanthropy; entrepreneurship; non-credit programs; among others.[20] Grants and contracts have provided the lifeblood for traditional research universities, but not so much for community colleges. This circumstance is beginning to change.

In the past two decades, community colleges have managed to convince lawmakers of the need to increase the percentage of federal grants and contracts awarded to community colleges. Most notable is their success in expanding funding for science, technology, engineering and mathematics, the so-called STEM fields, through the National Science Foundation (NSF). The Advanced Technology Education (ATE) program within NSF has experienced robust growth in recent years, and more community colleges are beginning to take advantage of federal funds to increase and expand their offerings in applied technology and related STEM fields. Following the terrorist attacks of 9/11, community-college leaders sought attention and support from federal homeland security agencies to create new partnerships for community college workforce training programs in the areas of airport security and screening, as well as first-responders and safety and rescue professionals. Such efforts have helped steer more grants and contracts to community colleges for important programs that ensure public safety, while at the same time elevating the visibility of community-college programs as important partners in the war on terrorism.

Earmarks

Community colleges have become more sophisticated in their targeting of federal dollars—a capability which has led to the creation of more federal grant and contract programs, for which community colleges are eligible to compete. Where grant and contract programs are insufficient to address specific needs, community-college presidents have engaged lobbyists to work the halls of Congress to obtain earmarks or other funds specifically geared to community-college programs and services.

The practice of earmarking funds within federal budgetary line items is not new—universities have used earmarks for years to fund laboratories, physical plants and performing-arts facilities. In fact, in 2009, there were an estimated 11,914 earmarks in the federal budget, for a total of over $20 billion.[21] For community colleges, this landscape is relatively new and uncharted and it may be changing faster than community colleges can tap into. Congress has begun restricting earmarks. Eliminating earmarks completely has become appealing to candidates running for political office, as a way to highlight the greed and self-serving interests of the political establishment. However, it is still necessary for community-college trustees and presidents to go to Washington, D.C., and work to convince their elected officials to support funds for college-specific programs and services, while also advocating on behalf of the comprehensive mission of community colleges.

Outsourcing

Another resource strategy worthy of attention in community colleges is outsourcing programs and services to vendors. Outsourcing can have dual benefits of reducing costs and boosting revenue. Ivy Tech Community College in Indiana—a thirty-campus network serving as the community college system for the state—released an announcement in August 2011 stating that:

[. . .] cost savings and revenue enhancement initiatives implemented over the last three fiscal years have resulted in $50.1 million in recurring annual savings, $7.4 million in one-time benefits and $19.3 million in future savings and increased revenue for the college. [22]

A portion of savings and revenue was attributed to Ivy Tech's contract with Follett Higher Education Group, which operates Ivy Tech's campus bookstores. By outsourcing campus bookstores, Ivy Tech helped save the college nearly $22.5 million over 3 years. [23] In addition to saving money, the bookstore contract also resulted in saving Ivy Tech students some $9.5 million in textbook expenses in 2011. [24] Ivy Tech has been able to use its statewide purchasing power to net savings on office equipment and furniture, all of which has reduced college costs while capping tuition and fees. While not new to community colleges, outsourcing is taking on new urgency as a way to lower expenses to lessen the impact of funding cuts. Outsourcing also increases value of services and programs available to students and the community, and strengthens the partnership between community colleges, the business community, and local employers.

Entrepreneurship

Innovation is becoming more than just a buzzword in community college development and resource strategy. As Mellow and Heelan point out, "if the trend in diminishing public support continues, it is likely that the range and financial contribution of these innovative forms or revenue generation will continue to proliferate." [25] As a result, community-college leaders are becoming more entrepreneurial—both in how they approach partnerships and how they lead and make decisions about resource allocations. Many colleges actively seek new and innovative partnerships and opportunities that stretch traditional notions of resource allocation and community partners.

The concept of the "entrepreneurial college" is becoming more prevalent and far-reaching. Community colleges are stepping up their efforts to become more entrepreneurial in relationships with area employers and schools. For instance, Northern Essex Community College in Massachusetts has encouraged its academic departments to develop entrepreneurial relationships with organizations off campus; for instance, campus departments have contracted with local high schools to provide courses in underutilized high-school classrooms. This strategy enables Northern Essex to meet course needs that would otherwise be nearly impossible due to space and facility constraints. The college also has negotiated a relationship with a local university to rent its unused classroom space to permit the university to offer an MBA degree on the Northern Essex campus.

Philanthropy

Philanthropy also is becoming a critical new resource partner for community colleges. With large and influential foundations such as the Bill & Melinda Gates Foundation, Lumina Foundation for Education, and the Ford, Kresge, Mott, and Hewlett foundations, to name a few, community colleges are becoming increasingly successful in procuring resources to do critically important work that targets a variety of social and educational imperatives. One such example of how philanthropy is working to leverage change and support innovation is the Achieving the Dream initiative:

> Conceived as an initiative in 2004 by Lumina Foundation and seven founding partner organizations, today, Achieving the Dream is the most comprehensive non-governmental reform movement for student success in higher education history. With more than 150 institutions, 100 coaches and advisors, and 15 state policy teams—working throughout 30 states and the District of Columbia—Achieving the Dream helps 3.5 million community college students have a better chance of realizing greater economic opportunity and achieving their dreams.[26]

Achieving the Dream has become an important strategy for community colleges, not only in serving disadvantaged students, but also in the application of data and data-driven decision making to guide development and growth of programs for disadvantaged populations. Such large-scale reform efforts in community colleges would not be possible without philanthropic support.

Going Green

Community colleges, like other sectors, are working to reduce energy costs and their carbon footprints on earth's atmosphere. Such efforts not only help the planet, but also reduce operational expenses while providing important learning opportunities for students. Kirkwood Community College in Iowa is one such example. Kirkwood joined several community colleges in expanding the benefits of wind-energy technology through its $5.2 million, 2.5-megawatt wind turbine. The benefits are many:

> In addition to generating about one-third of the college's electricity needs (saving the school hundreds of thousands of dollars each year), the turbine serves as a hands-on learning tool for students in the school's energy production and distribution technologies program.[27]

The Kirkwood Turbine provides "hands-on" training to students entering the field of alternative energy and wind technology. A growing number of community colleges are pursuing similar projects and initiatives to save on energy costs, thereby significantly reducing operational costs that lessen the impact of funding cuts.

College Foundation

The move to create and expand community college foundations is flourishing and helping colleges not only survive tough times, but thrive. The growth in number and sophistication of community college foundations is impressive. The Council for Resource Development (CRD), the professional development arm of community college grant and development officers, now serves 700 community colleges—nearly 59 percent of the nation's 1,200 community colleges.[28] The challenge for community-college foundations has been the need to forge better and closer links to their communities, as well as to area businesses and employers. Traditionally, higher-education development has focused heavily on alumni giving and alumni development. Because community-college students are vastly more mobile and have multiple alliances, keeping track of community-college alumni can present unique challenges.

Noncredit Programs

The growing prevalence of non-credit courses and programs within community colleges also is helping to contribute to the financial bottom line. Noncredit courses and programs range from skilled-labor content areas to paraprofessional and customized business programs to personal enrichment.[29] There is a paucity of national data relative to noncredit courses, and few matrices exist to examine their overall impact or effectiveness. However, interviews with business and college leaders suggest a high level of satisfaction with non-credit offerings.

For community colleges, noncredit courses are more readily initiated and delivered because they bypass the traditional and rather laborious process of academic review and accreditation peer review. Additionally, while full-time administrators are hired to oversee noncredit programs, adjunct or part-time faculty are employed to teach such courses.[30] This practice significantly lowers the overhead for such courses, increasing their revenue-generating prowess while at the same time reducing cost to students. The connection between non-credit and credit is not well-documented, but community college leaders are quick to point out the relationship between students who begin on the non-credit side of the institution and then transition to the credit courses.

RENEWING THE PUBLIC COMPACT

If community colleges are to reverse the trend in public financing and rebuild their relationships with government, boards and presidents will need to focus on accountability, transparency, and above all, a renewed focus on the nexus between what colleges provide, and their impact on local and state economies. The connection between educational attainment and earnings is well-understood and generally well-accepted. However, increasing pressure on state and local governments to balance public demand with diminishing revenue has led many to favor short-term reallocation over sustained long-term economic investment. It is akin to a form of madness seeping into the physiology of how resource decisions are made and implemented, leading many policymakers to ignore the relationship between sustained investment in community colleges on the one hand and the expansion of wealth (income earnings, job creation, and tax revenues) created as a result.

From Bad to Worse

The United States faces real and unforgiving economic challenges. Projections issued by the U.S. Bureau of Labor Statistics (BLS) speculate that 54.8 million jobs will need to be filled between now and 2020,[31] as economic shifts intensify. With the Baby Boom generation now reaching retirement age, the pressures on federal and state treasuries will intensify. At the same time, immigration and demographic shifts are reshaping the socioeconomic landscape, and with this reshaping will come demand for products, services, and postsecondary education. The BLS projections estimate that 18 percent of the new jobs will require at least an associate's degree—roughly the same percentage of jobs as those requiring doctoral, professional, or master's degrees. Stated differently, more than two-thirds of job growth in the next decade will require workers with at least two years of higher education as the basic entry requirement. Most of this growth in occupational demand will be local, suggesting that community colleges will be tasked with meeting the educational needs of the nation's future labor force.

Pressure for More

The pressure on community colleges to increase their emphasis and concentrate more resources on local and state-centered, careers and technical job preparation will not abate any time soon. The need to maintain access to technical programs for broad segments of the population and to deliver state-of-the-art training is growing. In an era of strained public resources, the politics of scarcity will continue to pit short-term funding priorities, which yield immediate and gratifying results, against longer term investments that yield deeper and less visible impacts. Given the rising stock of community colleges in the eye of the public, grant and contract programs have reached the threshold of an opportunity to be exploited.

THINGS MUST CHANGE

This dynamic of scarcity must change through public acknowledgment of the historical contribution of community colleges to the economic bottom line. As highlighted in chapter 1, the economic impact of community colleges and the education and training that our colleges provide is *impressive and pervasive*. One need only consult the Internet to find hundreds if not thousands of articles, news releases, and analytical reports and studies chronicling the economic impact of community colleges. For instance, a statewide economic impact report released in 2010 by the Texas Association of Community Colleges, *Moving Texas Forward*, found:

> Texas taxpayers see a rate of return of 6.9% on their investment in Texas Community Colleges and the Texas economy sees a total annual contribution of $1.6 billion from these institutions. Additionally, the report finds that every dollar of state and local tax money invested in the colleges today yields a cumulative of $28.00 in benefits that accrue to all Texas residents as added income and avoided social costs. [32]

The contribution to the state economy and to taxpayers measured through the fifty community college districts in Texas is compelling, but by no means unique to Texas. Such findings ought to be sufficient to sway policymakers to increase investment in community colleges. But the reality could not be more different, and the likelihood of continued scarcity remains squarely on the horizon.

For community colleges and the nation to emerge more prosperous from the recession, we would do well to remember Giuseppe Tomasi di Lampedusa's warning that began chapter 1—that "things must change if we expect things to remain the same." If the nation seeks to maintain historically held values of progress and opportunity, we must find new ways to break the destructive cycle of scarcity in order to build consensus around sustained investment in those sectors that have the greatest impact on the largest number of people. Community colleges are just such a sector.

Community colleges reach more deeply into our nation's social and economic fabric than any other postsecondary institution. They have the potential to strengthen human capital through education and training precisely targeted to local, state, and national workforce and economic priorities. I have an idea—a parable of sorts—for how we might unleash the power of community colleges in the future. But before we reach that final chapter, we need to take into consideration forces that are at the center of that power: educational attainment and student success of students and leadership for the future.

Chapter Five

Completion Matters

We seek to help an additional 5 million Americans earn degrees and certificates in the next decade. Not since the passage of the original GI Bill and the work of President Truman's Commission on Higher Education—which helped to double the number of community colleges and increase by seven-fold enrollment in those colleges—have we taken such a historic step on behalf of community colleges in America.[1]

SETTING THE CONTEXT

On July 14, 2009, President Barack Obama proposed his American Graduation Initiative (AGI) legislation on the campus of Macomb Community College in Warren, Michigan. In proposing the initiative, the president challenged the nation's community colleges to increase the number of degrees they award to Americans by five million by the year 2020. According to the Organization for Economic Cooperation and Development's (OECD) 2011–2012 Fact Book, the United States dropped to sixteenth place in the world, as measured by the number of adults aged twenty-five to thirty-four in the population who attained a college degree.[2]

The AGI represented a clarion call to arms, imploring community colleges to redouble their efforts to move more students successfully through the academic pipeline and on to degree completion. The Obama administration identified community colleges as the primary sector of higher education most likely to affect degree completion because of their ubiquitous presence in every community in the country and the far-reaching impact of their mode of education. The AGI proposed to provide the community college sector with the resources needed—some $12 billion—to close the degree-completion gap between the United States and other developed and developing nations within ten years.

In short order, the Bill & Melinda Gates Foundation, Lumina Foundation for Education, the National Governors Association, Complete College America, and numerous philanthropic organizations joined the college-completion movement, each setting goals and benchmarks to help community colleges invent, and equip programs and services to further college completion. In April 2010, six national community-college organizations issued an unprecedented manifesto, *Democracy's Colleges: A Call to Action*, committing each organization to focus more intensively on college completion.

Executed by executives of the American Association of Community Colleges, Association of Community College Trustees, the Center for Community College Student Engagement, the League for Innovation in the Community College, the National Institute for Staff and Organizational Development, and Phi Theta Kappa, *Democracy's Colleges* represented a unified message and commitment on behalf of institutions and leaders for the first time. Together, these six organizations encompass trustees, presidents, college administrators, faculty, students, and other stakeholders working to support the nation's community colleges. In essence, the call to action urged community colleges to adopt practices and strategies to increase by 50 percent the number of graduates by the year 2020,[3] well exceeding President Obama's challenge.

PRIORITY SHIFT

The 1944 GI Bill[4] enacted during World War II, and, later, the National Defense Education Act (in response to the Soviet Union's 1957 Sputnik launch), unleashed unparalleled public and governmental recognition of the role higher education played in national economic and security strategies. Both initiatives helped spawn new generations of college-going student cohorts. As a result, America emerged from economic stagnation immediately following World War II to become the most educated and prosperous nation on earth. Somewhere between U.S. economic Cold War dominance of the 1950s and the twin oil embargoes of the 1970s, the public emphasis on college degrees shifted, with degrees no longer recognized as elemental to national security, but rather as a pathway to income. College-degree attainment moved from being seen as a collective good to that of an individual good. In short, a college degree became and has remained synonymous with higher lifetime earnings—the price of admission to the American Dream—and not much else.

This shift in priorities led to pronounced economic and educational ineffi-ciencies, exacerbating college costs and diversifying the college-going popu-lation. In the minds of parents and students, the prioritization of college degrees diminished the perceived value of other occupational pathways through which community colleges have fought to establish legitimacy. These include vocational and technical education, career preparation, and apprenticeships and internships—programs that enable high school graduates to enter economically viable careers and job fields in which skills are para-mount to degrees. The percentage of Americans who completed college de-clined during this period, giving rise to growing concerns about student persistence, degree completion, and student success.

The emerging paradigm facing community college leaders is the need to balance degree attainment against policies that embrace pathways enabling learners to persist and obtain a measurable and meaningful benchmark—whether it be a degree, certificate, occupational training, skills acquisition, or a higher-paying job. Community colleges, which offer degrees, certificates, and workforce training and preparation, must balance goals of maintaining open access to postsecondary education with student success and a demon-strable form of completion. This shift in paradigms is controversial and the transition required of colleges is a delicate matter and must be made thought-fully and purposefully. We must remember that community colleges were created for the primary purpose of offering educational opportunity beyond high school to every U.S. citizen. Refocusing on what has been labeled with the shorthand "student success" means meeting the commitment to open access—a commitment not observed by four-year colleges and universities—but at the same time investing considerable research and resources in evaluat-ing students performance, accommodating their learning needs, and guiding them to the ultimate goal of attaining a degree. This is not easily done in today's complex higher education marketplace.

DEFINING COMPLETION

It is important that we recognize and embrace a broad definition of comple-tion and student success so as not to do a grave disservice to 1,200 commu-nity colleges with differing missions, governance structures, student popula-tions, and business and industry partnerships. Degree and/or certificate com-pletion, transfer to four-year institutions, gaining measurable skills for em-ployment or promotion, and higher income earnings need to be included as evidence of completion and student success. This is especially true for com-munity colleges, which offer a wide array of programs and services to respond to the multiplicity of constituency and community needs. The challenge is to maintain access while maintaining quality, improving student success, and increasing completion rates, all while containing costs.

United States Secretary of Education Arne Duncan perhaps best captured the situation while speaking to attendees at the National Historically Black Colleges and Universities Conference in 2009. Secretary Duncan spoke of the conundrum confronting higher-education leaders:

> Every college president and every governing board wants to simultaneously improve quality, increase access, and yet constrain costs. To college executives [these choices]—quality, access, and cost—often seem like mutually conflicting choices.[5]

Increasing graduation rates and improving student success will require multiple strategies and realignment within institutions. This work must be led by boards and administrators. It is critically important work that has been embraced by the Obama administration, higher-education associations, foundations, think tanks, and a host of related groups. Community colleges must be more intentional about student success and completion. Access to the doors of a college that does not culminate in demonstrable evidence of success is nothing short of an unproductive end.

A Difficult Proposition

Increasing college completion represents an especially difficult proposition for community colleges chiefly because of the diversity of student demographics. Currently, only 28 percent of first-time, full-time students seeking an associate's degree graduate with a degree or certificate within three years of enrollment.[6] Moreover, less than half (45 percent) of students who attended a community college with the goal of completing a degree or certificate actually did so after six years.[7] These data are in direct contradiction to student aspirations. Eighty-four percent of students who enroll at a community college do so with the expressed goal of earning an associate's degree.[8] There is a real disconnect between student aspirations and what students actually achieve. This constitutes an imbalance between intention and results, and the results unfortunately have profoundly negative consequences both for students and society as a whole.

Getting to the Finish Line

In *Crossing the Finish Line*,[9] William Bowen and his coauthors examined a number of issues related to college completion, particularly for at-risk students—a population that overwhelmingly attends community and technical colleges. Specifically, they examined dropout rates linked to race, gender, and socioeconomic status. Analyzing completion rates at twenty-one flagship public universities and four statewide systems of public higher education, the book follows the progress of the entering class of 1999—from entry to graduation, transfer, or withdrawal. The book cites strategies and promising approaches that can be employed to remedy the completion deficit.

First, transfer students, like those from community colleges, often perform much better than do "native" students because of greater interaction with faculty, or because they are more sharply focused on academic goals after transferring. This is confirmed by community college faculty and presidents, who are quick to regale interested observers with anecdotes about students who perform as well or better in universities counterpoints who began college careers at four-year colleges and universities. Second, student financial assistance makes a real difference in lessening economic barriers to college attendance and persistence. And third, creating a better system for matching students to institutions really matters as a strategy for increasing the number of completers. This last point is gaining traction because student success or failure is strongly correlated with directing students to the institution best suited to their needs, which in many cases may be the community or technical college, not a four-year college or university. An example would be the student who leaves a community college after completing only a few courses, but finds lucrative employment in an industry in which his or her newly acquired skills are valued. Failing to recognize what is most appropriate for individual students creates waste and inefficiency and, worse yet, represents a disservice to students and parents as goals and aspirations are thwarted.

WHAT WE KNOW

Strategies exist now that would enable community college boards and administrators to address student success and increase completion. During a Summit on Completion convened in October 2010 by the Association of Community College Trustees with the support of the Bill & Melinda Gates Foundation, Lumina Foundation for Education, and the College Board, community college trustees and presidents helped to identify a number of strategies that could increase student success and completion. The Summit on Completion took place over two days and included plenary lectures, as well as five topical work groups made up of the higher education leaders who were selected to participate.

Demand versus Resources

One Summit group focused on the mismatch between demand and resources, noting that "improving student completion will require fundamental restructuring, rather than piecemeal adjustments that often result in marginal efficiencies."[10] The recommendations covered a wide swath of current community college academic and administrative policies.[11] What is needed is a fundamental rethinking of goals and priorities related to community college degree and certificate attainment, and transfer to four-year baccalaureate colleges and university programs. These would include reexamining the targeting and allocation of financial resources such as student financial assistance, creating greater flexibility for community colleges in targeting dollars to incent student behavior and goal alignment, redoubling efforts to educate and inform students and parents about college financing options, and creating an appropriate rewards system for college faculty and administrators (as well as students) to facilitate completion.

Access and Completion

Another Summit group focused on the relationship between college access and college completion. Community colleges have been enormously successful in widening the doors to college for millions of Americans. Access without success, however, constitutes a broken promise. As the group noted, "linking access with completion will require a variety of approaches, including stronger alignment between K–12 curriculum and college requirements through structures as K–14/16 councils and programs including middle colleges and dual enrollment."[12] Speaking to issues of student engagement and acceleration, another group identified the necessity for reexamining methodologies to engage high-need student constituencies—underserved students, returning veterans, incarcerated individuals, and men of color—"to experience greater success in the community college setting."[13]

Connecting Educational Sectors

A fourth Summit group discussed partnerships to better connect community colleges within the K–16 pipeline. Participants agreed that community colleges must identify and expand connection points between themselves and the elementary- and secondary-school systems, as well as four-year colleges and universities within their service districts. Transparent data and information regarding pathways to community college, and what is takes to be successful, need to be made more readily available. Important for success is engaging community college trustees in the conversation about completion and student success, and their community peers in the conversation. The final Summit group explored the need for matrices to measure community college productivity. Discussants agreed that consistent, longitudinal data that acknowledge and conform to the complexities of community college missions are needed to inform policymakers and others about what community colleges can do, for whom, and to what end.

During a town hall meeting convened during the 2010 Association of Community College Trustees Leadership Congress that followed the Summit on Completion, numerous ideas were brought forth that mirror those being articulated and advocated by other policy analysts. The recommendations, which have been trumpeted by many others over the past several years, represent steps that community colleges can take to increase student success and completion. The challenge is to take what is known and work to bring these innovations and strategies to scale, allowing those innovations or strategies to become mainstream, resulting in greater uniformity across the community colleges.

ADDRESSING PREPARATION

In chapter 2, it was disclosed that 60 percent of students entering community colleges need at least one or more remedial (developmental) education courses in order to move on to postsecondary-level curricula and programs. In plain terms, the majority of community college enrollees need to be taught high school–level classes before they can even begin their higher-education careers. Furthermore, numerous studies have pinpointed the fact that less than one-quarter of the students taking their first remedial or developmental course successfully complete the course. This is a significant challenge for community colleges, and worse, it cuts off students' pathway to "the American Dream" even before they can get on the path. Specifically:

> Because too many students are not learning the basic skills needed to succeed in college or work while they are in high school, the nation loses more than $3.7 billion a year. This figure includes $1.4 billion to provide remedial education to students who have recently completed high school. In addition, this figure factors in the almost $2.3 billion that the economy loses because remedial reading students are more likely to drop out of college without a degree, thereby reducing their earning potential.[14]

The economic toll of a rising proportion of learners requiring remediation is vast, and it is troubling to governmental leaders—state and federal—who feel intensive pressure to continue to commit public dollars to education. Left unaddressed, developmental education programs might require more resources than some community colleges can commit in era of diminished public funding.

Remedial/Developmental Education

The "remedial" problem can involve misalignment between high school and community college curricula. Community colleges have admission standards. Entering students are tested by community colleges to assess "college readiness." The tests are designed to measure whether students possess the core competencies to achieve at a college level. Most students have graduated from high schools with diplomas; others may have been out of school for long periods, or are seeking to reenter the workplace or upgrade their skills. For the students recently graduated from high school, imagine the rude awakening when assessment results reveal that they must enter a remedial or development course because they lack "college-level" skills. For students who have been out of the college environment for many years, it may come as less of a shock, but it must be demoralizing and perhaps a financial blow to learn that they must temporarily postpone or delay pursuing higher education or higher-level training while they take remedial courses to get up to speed. Money is not in ample supply for many community college students, and having to confront unexpected and prolonged expenses for pre-college courses can be enough to discourage students from pursuing higher education.

Aligning for Results

Student success can be improved by aligning community college assessment exams with high school curricula—especially in mathematics and English reading and comprehension. It is incumbent upon community colleges to share their expectations and standards for college-level proficiency with high-school teachers and administrators. Blaming high schools for not preparing students for study at the community college is not an appropriate approach to solving the problem. Bringing the teaching of mathematics and English reading and comprehension into alignment from high school to community college represents fertile ground, for both fostering student success and, more importantly, lessening the economic inefficiencies that result from academic failure.

Understanding Pathways to Success

Community-college faculty and administrators should routinely reach out and engage their peers in K–12 schools—elementary through high school—in dialogue about what it takes to succeed at a community or technical college. The same should apply to community-college boards and school boards. Boards should meet regularly to discuss best practices and innovative approaches for better aligning curricula so that more students will graduate from high school college-ready. Barriers that impede concurrent enrollment need to be eliminated. Concurrent enrollment has the dual benefits of both preparing students for and accelerating progress to completion, ultimately reducing the need for remedial or developmental courses.

Creating Seamless Systems

As with aligning K–12 and community-college curricula and standards, seamless student transfer and articulation agreements between community colleges and four-year universities are needed. While a growing number of community colleges are offering baccalaureate degrees, partnerships with neighboring universities offer robust economies of scale that serve the twin purposes of extending students' degree options while at the same time creating greater resource efficiencies. Transfer policies and accreditation standards need to be better aligned and mutually reinforcing among institutions. It is counterintuitive that regional accrediting bodies, which accredit both four-year and two-year institutions within the same region, effectively sanction the practice of making students who transfer between institutions retake courses previously completed for credit. This suggests that while accredited by the same body, institutions are inherently unequal relative to the value of lower division courses. If the goal of fostering persistence and success is paramount, this practice needs to be addressed and resolved. In Florida, the use of common course-numbering systems represents just one of several innovative practices:

> [A] key component of Florida's K–20 seamless system of articulation[:] . . . The system provides a database of postsecondary courses at public vocational-technical centers, community colleges, universities, and participating nonpublic institutions. The assigned numbers describe course content to improve research, assist program planning, and facilitate the transfer of students. [15]

By agreement, the four-year universities and community colleges in Florida essentially have agreed that "College-Level Math 101" is essentially the same course regardless of what institution offers the course. Solutions like Florida's common course-numbering system are needed to enhance the objective of making students progress from two-year to four-year institutions seamless.

Better Outcomes

In addition to aligning high school and community college curricula, developmental classes could be made to be more intensive and better targeted to students through pinpoint assessment of skills and academic goals and aspirations. In reality, tracking student cohorts is less important than focusing on identifying what students really need and providing it more efficiently. More developmental students need "curriculum chunks" as opposed to entire semester courses. Ascertaining student deficiencies with greater degrees of accuracy would serve to "fast track" students through the developmental cycle, allowing them to move more rapidly into postsecondary courses and programs.

An example of how community colleges can fast track first-time students through developmental programs is the Math Jam program at Pasadena City College in the Pasadena Area Community College District in Southern California.[16] Math Jam is a two-week, free summer program that exposes entering students to mathematics and success in a low-stress environment before students arrive on campus. Essentially a "transition to college" program, Math Jam provides innovative instruction in mathematics and student orientation and support services designed to increase student success and academic achievement. Since its inception in 2006, 842 students have completed Math Jam. College officials hope to continue to expand Math Jam in future years to achieve higher levels of student success and completion while also reducing the need for developmental mathematics courses for entering first-time students. Math Jam is a reminder that community colleges can realign their approach to remedial education programs in order to eliminate duplication and create more seamless pathways. There is no need to reinvent the wheel when it comes to serving students well—assessing their academic needs more precisely allows forward progress for a greater number of students.

Faculty Development

When it comes to developmental instruction, community colleges should be mindful of relegating the teaching of such courses to part-time faculty or adjuncts. Too often, these instructors lack classroom experience or effective pedagogical skill to teach developmental courses and engage students appropriately. Developmental education students often need as much psychological triage as they do basic-skills instruction. Students are understandably discouraged when they must take developmental courses. They lack confidence, and oftentimes the motivation to succeed. Faculty need to be skilled with the knowledge and experience sufficient to restore a student's confidence by helping the student see his or her way through the course and beyond. Instructors who teach students in developmental courses are meritorious people—they need specialized teaching and intervention skills. Numerous community-college programs have been initiated to sharpen faculty and adjunct-faculty skills and promote higher levels of student achievement. For instance, Montgomery County Community College, just outside Philadelphia, Pennsylvania, has engaged faculty to redesign and rethink the college's teaching approach to remedial and developmental courses.[17] By enabling faculty closest to the problems and issues facing developmental students to participate in the solution, new approaches were instituted and faculty retrained. Student-success rates in developmental programs have increased as a result.

STARTING OFF RIGHT

Most students come to community college with success and/or completion as their goal. Failure is not among the goals students cite for enrolling in a college. Yet, too often, students come to college ill-equipped to navigate the academic environment. Frequently, students have not declared academic goals or academic majors. Most have little to no understanding about course sequences, prerequisites, and general education requirements. This is by no means unique to community colleges. Four-year colleges and universities are just as, if not more, mysterious to entering students, especially those without clear academic goals. As Kay McClenney, director of the Center for Community College Student Engagement at the University of Texas at Austin, is fond of saying, "students don't do optional"; that is, given a choice, students opt out of orientation or advising services when they are not required by the institution. Institutions that require new student orientation sometimes involve parents in seminars and programs designed to broaden their understanding of how to help their children succeed in college. These orientation programs help to ensure that students begin on the right path—a path that needs to be continuously reinforced as students advance through the institution.

Student Orientation

If the nation's elite colleges and universities can require participation in extensive new-student orientation programs that acquaint incoming students with virtually every aspect of the institutional experience, thereby enhancing their understanding and ability to navigate the academy, so too should community colleges. By focusing on new student orientation, Chipola College in Florida has been able to achieve measurable effects on student knowledge of what it takes to succeed in college and improve graduation rates. The college created mandatory faculty workshops and paid summer institutes to engage faculty in activities to elevate student success and completion. The college also instituted a number of other reforms including mandatory entering-student orientation and counseling and revamping college curriculum guides as "academic plans" to enhance completion.[18] Tragically, not enough community colleges offer new-student orientation programs or services because, truthfully, they seldom have the resources—both human and financial—to implement or sustain such programs. This is a challenge to be sure, but investing resources in students who do not persist constitutes a larger financial drain on the institution. The return on new-student orientation may well eclipse the costs in the long run, and certainly will increase the likelihood of student success and completion. If community colleges are serious about student success, resources must be brought to bear to support strategies that assist students in making the right choices and mining institutional resources that will help them succeed.

Eliminating Institutional Barriers

As with new student orientation programs, students need assistance in breaking down institutional barriers and avoiding administrative red tape. Our colleges need to create simplified education plans that focus on student success and lessen institutional barriers wherever possible. Additionally, students who have completed a significant number of credits should be identified and encouraged to finish. Students should not leave an institution without evidence of completion, especially for those who are only a few credits shy of earning a credential. In other words, colleges should not ignore the "low-hanging fruit" that will help boost graduation and transfer rates.

Financing College Persistence

The U.S. Department of Education's National Center for Education Statistics 2009 survey revealed that one-third of students enrolled in community colleges received federal financial assistance, principally through the Federal Pell Grant program.[19] Pell Grants are needs-based grants of up to (as of the current 2011–2012 award year) $5,550 per year, which do not have to be repaid and which represent a growing commitment to reduce economic barriers to pursuing undergraduate postsecondary education. But Pell Grants are not the only form of public support available to low-income and economically disadvantaged students.

According to Single Stop USA, a not-for-profit organization committed to reducing poverty and increasing educational attainment, more than $65 billion in various forms of public assistance go unspent each year. Some of this assistance would permit more low-income and economically disadvantaged students to access community colleges, and begin a journey to self-empowerment and improved quality of life.

Single Stop USA, in partnership with the Association of Community Colleges Trustees, is working with community colleges to increase access and persistence by helping students to obtain public assistance for which they are already eligible. Additionally, Single Stop USA works with community colleges to further enhance institutional capacities around needed support services to sustain financially vulnerable students on a pathway to success. According to Single Stop USA, this strategy is based on the following:

To ensure a holistic approach to the diversity of barriers that students face, Single Stop provides comprehensive social, legal and financial services—all free to the student—and uses existing state and federal resources as a proxy for stipends that have been shown to help students stay in school through completion. As an intermediary, Single Stop also builds the capacity of its community college partners and provides valuable resources, training, and technical support while working closely with existing initiatives to enhance available services and ensure coordinated case management. Using a proprietary technology platform akin to Turbo Tax, the Benefits Enrollment Network (BEN), Single Stop Coordinators (fully funded staff lines at each college with which we partner) verify client eligibility for a wide spectrum of benefits, tax credits and services, thus achieving in approximately 15 minutes what frequently takes weeks or even months to complete. Coordinators then provide comprehensive counseling and supportive wrap-around services to help clients navigate the system and effectively utilize the benefits and services they receive.[20]

Groundbreaking in the simplicity it offers students, Single Stop USA builds the capacity of its college partners using highly trained staff and proprietary technology to provide students with a single access point for the benefits and services for which they are eligible. These include supports such as tax credits, public health insurance, legal assistance and financial counseling—programs and services that frequently make the difference for students who are otherwise forced to choose between groceries and graduation. Since the inception of the organization's partnership with ACCT over two years ago, Single Stop USA has provided services to more than 30,000 community-college students across the country, helping them to access more than $70 million worth of benefits and services. Even more compelling, however, is early evidence suggesting that students who receive Single Stop USA services are more likely to persist than those who do not.[21]

Financial Assistance Lifeline

Providing financial assistance, whether through traditional means such as Pell Grants or innovative new models such as Single Stop USA to leverage public assistance and tax benefits, represents a vital lifeline for low-income and disadvantaged students. But too often, students and community colleges do not take full advantage of financial support mechanisms to increase persistence and accelerate completion—often because they simply do not know that the resources exist. For instance, students need to know that, in some cases, increased financial aid might supplement or even supplant part-time work, allowing them to pursue more credit hours, increase the likelihood of completing. Too many students erroneously believe that they must work full or part-time in order to cover their tuition when in fact they might qualify for needs-based aid, thereby avoiding the competing priorities of work and study which retard persistence and completion. Educating students about financial aid options is part of fostering access and student success. Community colleges should continue to be innovative with respect to introducing students to financial mechanisms that are available to enhance persistence and completion.

Behind the "Eight Ball"

Many community colleges are re-examining policies and practices that create disincentives or real barriers to student success. For example, allowing students to register late for classes—sometimes several weeks into the semester—creates a "behind-the-eight-ball" effect for students by placing them at a four-to-six week disadvantage in the course curriculum. Too often, students cannot make up the missing weeks and fail as a result. Late registration has been employed by community colleges to increase access and allow for greater student choice and flexibility. However, allowing students to begin their college studies four to six weeks after the start of a semester virtually guarantees partial or total failure. There is a lot of common sense to this argument. If students begin their academic pursuits already behind, why should it come as any surprise that many never make it to the finish line? If community college leaders are serious about increasing student success, then they must accept that allowing late registration is an immediate impediment to persistence for a great number of students, regardless of models and paradigms that have been employed for decades. For instance, York Technical College in South Carolina eliminated late registration in 2009.[22] According to the York course guide, "the Late Registration period is three days immediately preceding any semester or mini-session. After a semester or mini-session begins, students may not register for those sessions."[23] In order to accommodate students who cannot register on time, the college offers some of its more popular courses in collapsed formats of eight to twelve weeks, later in the semester.

Paying to Graduate?

A growing number of community college presidents identified the issue of the graduation fee as an impediment to completion and to students obtaining a credential. Because community college students have such limited financial resources, they sometimes forgo paying the graduation fee, thereby failing to obtain a diploma—even though they have completed the requisite number of credits entitling them to the degree. Worse still, many institutions require students to apply to receive their degrees upon completion. Given today's marketplace, community colleges need to respond aggressively to student needs and interest by finding every means available to ensure that every student who has earned the degree automatically receives the diploma.

Increase Rigor/Requirements

More controversial strategies involve increasing the number of college pre-requisites and increasing academic rigor. These can be debilitating and problematic and unconstructive if not done in a thoughtful manner because their net effect inherently is to reduce access and create barriers to success. The better idea is to focus energy on assuring that students enter programs with the correct preparation and skill sets, and engage them in programs with sufficient rigor that enable them to experience early success and continue their pathway to and through upper-division courses.

NATIONAL RECOGNITION

During the White House Summit on Community Colleges in 2010, President Obama announced that "the Aspen Institute and several leading foundations are launching a competitive prize for community-college excellence. It's going to shine a spotlight on community colleges delivering truly exceptional results—places that often don't get a lot of attention, but make a significant difference in their students' lives."[24] The creation of a national prize recognizing the efforts of community colleges was unprecedented and set ripples through the community-college world. After more than a year of intensive evaluations of college performance data, the Aspen Institute announced on December 12, 2011 the first-ever ten finalists for the Aspen Prize for Community College Excellence: [25]Lake Area Technical College in South Dakota; Miami Dade College in Florida; Mississippi Gulf Coast Community College; Mott Community College in Michigan; Northeast Iowa Community College; Santa Barbara City College in California; Southwest Texas Junior College; Valencia College in Florida; Walla Walla Community College in Washington, and West Kentucky Community and Technical College. Valencia College was announced as the winner of the Aspen Prize, and with it a check for $600,000. By announcing Valencia as the winner:

> Aspen officials noted that more than half, 51 percent, of the college's full-time students, most of whom pursue associate degrees, complete them within three years of enrolling. That's a graduation rate significantly higher than the national average of 39 percent at community colleges. Valencia offers more than 700 courses a term to its 50,000 for-credit students. [26]

To determine its winner, the Aspen Institute developed a series of matrices based on indicators such as completion and transfer rates, labor market outcomes, learning outcomes, and equitable outcomes. After data analysis was completed, Aspen officials conducted site visits to the institutional finalist to observe and learn firsthand about efforts designed to increase student success and completion. Another Aspen Prize will be awarded in 2012. Ultimately, the Aspen Prize represents appreciation for and investment in community colleges, and also represents a major motivation for community colleges to invest greater resources in performance analysis and outcomes.

WHAT IT TAKES

The renewed emphasis on student success and completion is gaining greater acceptance in community colleges. Getting to the president's completion goals is arduous and requires courage to confront hard realities about students and teaching and the learning environment in community colleges. Shifting the paradigm toward student success and completion requires a level of partnership among many players. Community-college governing boards must take the lead in precisely defining student success and completion in the context of their own institutions. Once defined, boards should place high priority on assessing and highlighting student success and completion on board meeting agenda. This would send a powerful signal to audiences that the board is serious about making completion a priority and is focusing college resources and energies on equipping students for success.

Boards should work in partnership with the president to set realistic goals and expectations around student success and completion. A culture of evidence should be developed in every institution, which starts with the board and its ability to receive data regularly on student achievement and success. Data on student persistence, completion, transfer, dropouts, and the like, need to be disaggregated in ways that allow for a clear understanding of what is transpiring within various cohorts. Only then can boards begin to hold institutions accountable for increasing student persistence and completion and foster the culture of evidence needed to sustain success over the long run. Among the distinguishing factors of community colleges, including Aspen Prize–winner Valencia College, is that the presidents of colleges that have leveraged significant gains in student success and completion have served ten or more years at their current institutions. Committing to and sustaining progress in student success and completion takes perseverance and time.

Helping students cross the finish line with a degree or transfer to a four-year college or university is one of many pathways to success. We need more achievers in America and we need more individuals with the skills and knowledge necessary to continuously stoke the nation's economic engines. The sustained focus on increasing student success and completion matters. Finishing what we start matters. Intervening against failure matters. Far more effort is needed to recalibrate community-college programs and services to both incent and deliver on the promise of access leading to measurable and meaningful results for individuals and society. In the nation's zeal to expand college access, we have continually equated college degrees with higher income and quality of life without helping individuals understand which institutions would best foster their success and economic prospects. As a result, an imbalance has been created that is becoming more manifest and is hurting America's economic progress.

We need to refocus and reset our sights on what matters to our economy now and where we need to make strategic and meaningful policy changes that will unleash the intrinsic power of community colleges to help restore the balance. America needs to recommit itself to student success; the country needs to commit to building and sustaining a culture of evidence that will re-engage the public sector in ways that foster increased investment in, and recognition of, the critical and inseparable link between educational attainment and economic and national security. Success in this effort should be seen as non-negotiable. Community colleges are resolved when it comes to innovation. Let us embrace the innovators.

Chapter Six

Leadership Imperatives

Better is possible. It does not take genius. It takes diligence. It takes moral clarity. It takes ingenuity. And, above all, it takes a willingness to try. [1]

LEADERS FOR NEW TIMES

Today's higher education enterprise—including community colleges—is more complex than at any time in history. Higher education has become more market driven and has been forced to respond to ever-changing student needs. Since World War II, the nation has embarked on a strategy to make higher education more accessible, and through federal student-assistance programs, more affordable. This has led both to the "democratization" of student enrollments and a high degree of elasticity of demand for postsecondary education at all levels. As a result, the number of community colleges in the United States has more than quadrupled since the early 1960s, creating many new opportunities not only for students, but also for jobs—including many more opportunities for presidential leadership in community colleges. The expansion of community colleges has created a challenge of assuring that the leader pipeline is sufficient to serve the current and projected needs of colleges. The longstanding, tried-and-true principles of leadership must now be adapted to suit an ever-changing economic climate and a challenging learning environment.

The growing complexity of higher-education programs and services is requiring community college presidents to confront new challenges, and with those challenges, master new skill sets that go beyond the traditional skills once sufficient to cement the role of presidents as primary academic leaders. New skills include strategic planning, resource management, strategy formulation, navigating new technologies—to support campus operations and services while also adapting to rapidly changing student learning styles—understanding the impact of regulations and reporting requirements, accountability and outcomes assessment, and other skills focusing on specialized knowledge and its application.

TODAY'S LEADERS

The data on today's college presidents do not bode well for the future for those who hope that the status quo in community colleges will continue. According to a report by the American Council on Education (ACE), almost half of college and university presidents are over sixty-one years of age,[2] meaning that there will be significant turnover in presidencies in the next ten to fifteen years. The ACE report goes on to highlight the relative dearth of presidents with diverse backgrounds, sharply contrasting with growing institutional and student diversity. A report released in March 2012 by ACE, *The American College President*, shows little movement toward diversifying the presidency between 2006 and 2011. While the number of women presidents increased overall, the number of presidents of color is largely unchanged over the past several years.[3]

This suggests that as community college student enrollments continue to become more diverse, presidents and boards need strategies for taking full advantage of the extraordinary opportunities to infuse the presidency with individuals of diverse perspectives and experience. It is critical to ensure that the presidential pipeline is rich with talented individuals, who are ready to assume the reins of community colleges. And the pipeline will need to reach individuals outside of traditional academic circles, as studies also point to the fact that only one-quarter of chief academic officers (vice presidents, deans, provosts, and other senior staff) indicate their interest to aspire to the presidency. This presents real obstacles for community colleges and their ability to identify and nurture prospective candidates for the presidency. If not from within the college, then where will colleges find future presidents—and how will the influence of "outsider" leaders affect the college?

Past is *Not* Prologue

The traditional career ladder for aspiring community college presidents has typically involved moving from being an instructor, to dean or department head, to academic leader, to vice president, and eventually on to the presidency. This trajectory takes many years to complete and sometimes involves moving from one institution to another or from state to state, where opportunities are more abundant for gaining a foothold on the presidential career ladder. With community colleges relying more heavily on part-time or adjunct faculty, the prospects for adjuncts to learn and transition to leadership positions within the community college are significantly diminished.

Community college presidents report that fewer of their vice presidents appear interested in or willing to submit themselves to the presidency, presumably because the demands relative to time, professional investment, visibility, leadership and the like of the presidency have changed dramatically. A number of leadership programs, focusing on preparing PhD or EdD candidates for academic and administrative positions have been established over the years, primarily at research universities, to prepare and position the new generation of presidents. However, many of those programs have been collapsed or reorganized within schools of education or university departments, diminishing the emphasis on presidential leadership and the capacity to meet growing demand for leaders with traditional academic credentials. Regardless, the impending retirement wave suggests that current leadership programs are insufficient to grow the ranks of presidential leader. The "graying" of the presidency portends a scarcity of presidential talent when new talent will be more critical than ever to keep community colleges on an even keel through the turbulent waters of declining public resources and growing demands for programs and services.

Leadership Diversity

The nation's community colleges can ill afford a leadership deficit at a time when strong leadership is increasingly more critical to the future of community colleges. With a growing list of challenges and changes in the mix of presidential competencies, community colleges will need to refocus leadership recruitment in ways that will allow boards to be open to individuals of differing professional backgrounds, while also broadening their recruitment efforts. Specifically, community college boards will need to redouble their focus on identifying visionary future leaders by being intentional with regard to potential leaders who have more diverse educational backgrounds and professional experiences falling outside of the academy. This might include looking to nonprofit organizations, philanthropic entities, business, government, community-based groups, and others, where individuals with exceptional leadership skills can be found.

A major roadblock for boards looking outside the traditional pipeline for institutional leadership is the discomfort that comes from going against the grain of traditional academic and cultural norms boards have tended to honor in recruiting senior institutional leaders. Most boards embrace, and are accustomed to, hiring college presidents with doctoral degrees, and significant teaching and administrative experience informed by and shaped through years spent in higher education. Board discomfort is often reinforced be by fears that faculty will reject leaders from outside academic ranks. Boards need to be open and transparent with regard to presidential searches in order to build acceptance and support from faculty and the community. Their rationale for looking for exceptionally talented and diverse leaders from outside higher education should be driven by a desire to perform due diligence, in which the overall needs of the institution are carefully weighed and measured. Boards should assume leadership by engaging faculty and staff in moving the institution forward collaboratively.

Balancing Act

In their book *Community Colleges on the Horizon: Challenge, Choice, or Abundance*, coauthors Richard Alfred, Christopher Shults, Ozan Janquette, and Shelley Strickland provide a highly relevant and focused list of leadership traits: visioning; inventiveness; smart choices; balancing ideas with execution; sense making; relating; inclusiveness; creating and managing change; simplicity; identifying and multiplying talent; how to create and use networks; urgency; integrity and commitment; and balancing extrinsic and intrinsic motivation.[4] Many of these same characteristics are cited throughout the wealth of work on leadership, including college and university leadership.

Working with these attributes, it is important to delineate key characteristics of the twenty-first-century college leader. First, leaders must balance vision with pragmatism.[5] The leaders who will help community colleges navigate the future will be able to articulate that future while remaining realistic about what can be achieved, and at what pace. It's about scaling one's vision of the future in ways that allow success to flow systematically— not overcommitting and then failing to deliver. The next generation of community college presidents will need to be clear-eyed about what is achievable and, more importantly, able to educate and inform their boards about resources and alignment with the mission and community. At the same time, community college presidents will need to engage key institutional constituencies in a vision of possibilities, engaging them as co-collaborators, invested in the vision. As Alfred and colleagues point out, "leaders who are skilled in visioning are able to get staff excited about their conception of the future while inviting them to sharpen the image."[6] Leadership is never effective in a vacuum—leaders are those who inspire others to embrace the vision and make it their own in ways that ensure success and forward progress.

The 1988 landmark report *Building Communities: A Vision for a New Century* expressed similar notions in a straightforward and powerful vision about the community college presidency:

> Building communities requires creative leaders, and the president is key. The president must move the college beyond day-to-day operations. He or she must call upon the community of learning to affirm tradition, respond to challenges, and create inspiring visions for the future. To do this, the president must be able to collaborate, bring together various constituencies, build consensus, and encourage others within the college community to lead as well. [7]

As it looked foward to the new millennium, the Commission on the Future of Community Colleges' *Building Communities* was remarkably on point. The commission predicted that by the year 2000, community college presidents "increasingly would need to be coalition builders."[8] The commission's reasoning was that given the growing numbers of constituencies served by community colleges, presidents would have to learn to reach out, communicate, and engage more broadly to connect the colleges more tightly to their communities and stakeholders. This has become far more critical today than ever before. Community-college presidents now invest a significant amount of their time and personal capital identifying, building, and nurturing the partnerships necessary to enable their institutions to remain dynamic and relevant to community needs. Regardless of credentials, all qualified candidates for a community-college presidency in the new millennium need to be willing and eager to dedicate most of their time and their energy to the college while at the helm.

In Loco Patronus[9]

One of the important challenges facing community-college presidents is the need to spend more time away from the campus in order to solicit outside resources, advocate for policies, or tend to the 24-7 demands of supporting the mission of their institutions. In other words, a president must "have a presence but lead from a distance."[10] Today's challenges demand that community-college presidents have a strong presence within the institution, but delegate more to senior administrators in order to maintain an equally strong presence and visibility outside the institution. As Alfred and colleagues write, "leadership is about identifying and multiplying talent."[11] Effective community college presidents have the ability to identify, groom, encourage, and position individuals to assume greater leadership within the institution— to serve as *in loco patronus*—in place of the president when necessary.

Creating a senior leadership team to act on the president's behalf is critical to the success of any college. Likewise, it is incumbent upon the president to educate the governing board about the value of having such a team, and the reasons that compel its creation and continuing presence. Community-college boards need to be supportive and understanding of the president's senior management and academic team. It should never be the case that community-college boards fail to grasp the reasons why their presidents need to spend increasing amounts of time off campus, or on travel. The president has a responsibility to work the board to create not only an understanding of what necessitates time away, but also an awareness of the need to support the senior team and its development as part of continuity and effective functioning.

STAKES ARE HIGHER

Community-college presidents are dealing with new imperatives and increasing external pressure. The student-success-and-completion movement that began gaining prominence in late 2009 continues to gain speed and urgency on campuses. Coincidentally, this "call to arms" for completion is occurring at the same time that community colleges have seen double-digit enrollment gains while public funding has been declining. The stakes are elevating for community colleges, their boards and presidents. How well boards and presidents react and implement changes will, to some degree, influence senior administrators' choices about whether to pursue the presidency. In short, the stakes are higher now than at any time in the past for community college leaders. How well leaders and boards model their behavior and get things done will either encourage or discourage internal candidates from pursuing opportunities to lead an institution in the future.

Shifting Skill Sets

The skill sets needed by community-college presidents are evolving and ever-changing, yet core and essential skills remain the same The real challenge to existing skill sets is the speed with which issues come to the fore, requiring immediate attention, integration, and response. No, surprisingly, presidents frequently report that there is never enough money to respond to program and service needs of students, businesses, and the community in general. The American Association of Community Colleges, with the support of the W. K. Kellogg Foundation, developed an inventory of six "core competencies" needed by community college presidents. Released in 2005, those competencies were:

1. Organizational Strategy;
2. Resource Management;
3. Communication;
4. Collaboration;
5. Community College Advocacy; and
6. Professionalism [12]

Organizational strategy requires that presidents be strategic with respect to moving their institutions forward, assuring student success and community responsiveness, and using data to ensuring institutional accountability. Resource management involves the securing and allocation of resources to protect institutional assets and assure fiscal solvency. Resource management also extends to time management and organizational and reporting hierarchies to assure efficient and responsive college operations. Presidents must be extraordinary communicators. They must articulate a vision for the institution, while also engaging and enlisting support internally throughout the institution and externally throughout the community and among key stakeholders. Collaboration is equally important for building a supportive and cooperative environment within the college—an environment that embraces and fosters diversity, student learning, and other priorities, and which also advances the college mission. Advocating for their colleges is an important role for presidents, although this is one presidential role that must be coordinated and operate in concert with boards. Presidents are the visible leaders of their institutions and are well-positioned to be champions of student learning and public-policy favorable to the college, and engaging stakeholders in support of the college mission. Lastly, presidents set the professional tone within their institutions. They must model behavior that is ethical, fair, open and honest, while encouraging these behaviors within the institution.

Entrepreneurship is Essential

Informal conversations with community-college presidents reveal that many feel the need to be better entrepreneurs, experienced fundraisers, adept at crisis management, savvy financial managers, masters of media relations, and skilled at enabling student success. Presidents must embrace the new world of entrepreneurship, as well as be entrepreneurial in their own leadership styles. Entrepreneurship is the thread that has bound up the nation's tapestry and led us to greatness. Entrepreneurs and risk-takers carved the path in transforming our nation from an agrarian confederation of states to an industrialized superpower that redefined what was possible in the world. The newly "flattened" world economy, described by *New York Times* writer Thomas Friedman, brought about by broadband and wireless technologies that power everything from laptop computers to smart phones to iPods®, iPads®, Nooks®, and Kindles®, has seamlessly connected people and communities across the globe. Entrepreneurs today neither adhere to national boundaries nor are constrained by them. Such is the transformative power of broadband. In short, the entrepreneurial spirit is freer to express itself today than at any other time in human history.

Today's community-college presidents and those who aspire to the presidency must embrace the reality that entrepreneurship matters and must become "part and parcel" of the leadership toolkit. Students are more demanding and more consumer-driven than at any time in our history. For example, while broadband technology has made communication faster and easier than ever for presidents and for colleges to interact with students, students too can interact more easily with a larger array of institutions, including for-profit colleges and universities, who also compete for enrollments. Colleges need to be more creative and entrepreneurial in their approach to the market and radically change marketing paradigms, curricula, and campus services, office hours, etc. The changing environment requires that community-college presidents work with their boards to understand, adapt, and implement a more entrepreneurial culture throughout the college. The culture must embrace risk-taking and innovation—it must tolerate mistakes and missteps if innovation is to be unleashed. To meet changing demands, while at the same time sustaining high performance, will require more than sleight of hand—it will demand presidential leadership that transforms the traditional to the contemporary through innovation and entrepreneurial vision.

Fundraising

Community-college presidents must be more aggressive in looking for new sources of funding to support their institutions. Anecdotally, community-college presidents tell me that that they devote somewhere around 40 percent of their professional time to multiple forms of fundraising. Traditionally, community colleges have been at a disadvantage when it comes to raising funds. The community-college model presents some inherent challenges in this regard. For example, the diversity of the community-college student population and the transient nature of students "swirling" in and out of college, often without obtaining a degree or certificate, have undermined the success of traditional alumni-giving programs in community colleges. Alumni giving programs have been the "bread and butter" of traditional higher-education private giving and resource-development strategies. While the number of community-college foundations has grown to meet increasing resource needs, community colleges as a sector fall well short of traditional colleges and universities when it comes to leveraging private funds. Where once fund-raising skills and experience were minimally important for presidents, in today's world they have become a necessity—an essential skill for ensuring long-term stability of the college.

Handling Crisis

Presidents report that they need better preparation for dealing with the inevitable crises that will befall the institutions. Leaders need exacting skills for managing crises when they strike, fostering communication and transparency, and resolving current crises while building an infrastructure to prevent future crises. Knowledge about prevailing laws and jurisdictional responsibilities must be assimilated and understood. Issues of liability may extend beyond the narrow confines of campus property lines. Media coverage is 24-7 and instantaneous, giving leaders little room to delay public statements or to correct hastily given comments or misinformation released at the height of confusion. The president must appear in control, able to assume management and response and reassure constituencies, both internal and external. And above all else, presidents must work with and prepare the governing board for the eventuality of crisis by formulating policy that strengthens institutional response while preserving the credibility of the institution and its leadership. Numerous organizations and public and private entities exist that provide information, sample policies and disaster preparedness assessments. There is little reason why a college should be caught unprepared in today's litigious environment.

Financial Management

Funds to support community college programs and services are becoming mixed in origin and as a proportion of college operating and capital budgets. Understanding and managing the maze of college resources is becoming more closely tied to changing institutional priorities and incenting cultural and administrative behavioral shifts. Presidents today must be adept when it comes to managing changing financial conditions and financial oversight. On top of managing college finances, leaders must be aware of requirements related to federal, state and local auditing and accounting standards, institutional tax returns, and the growing need for transparency and accountability in all matters related to fiscal oversight. Should any request be made for financial information, the president should have more than a cursory knowledge of where the college stands and should be able to produce accurate and up-to-date financial information at a moment's notice. Because community colleges are state and local entities, the mechanism for funding operations and capital projects varies. What is permissible in some states is measurably different in other states. Frequently, presidents must be well-versed generalists in the areas of non-profit accounting, budgeting and financial management, auditing, and financial reporting requirements. They must also be able to communicate with sound judgment and with authority about all of these matters as the primary responsible party for the institution.

Media Relations

As mentioned relative to crisis management, leaders need to maintain a higher level of sophistication and effectiveness when it comes to managing the news cycle for institutions. Presidents often are the most visible and recognizable college representatives within their communities. Today, they live under a microscope and privacy is a luxury. Even on vacation, presidents sometimes are subject to recognition by the media and their activities reported to the public—sometimes antagonistically and without due cause. Where they shop, the cars they drive, their homes, recreational habits, and the like become fodder for public consumption by the media. Presidential compensation and benefits packages are often assessed publicly. On a positive note, presidents who understand the media and news cycle are less likely to become victims to malicious character attacks or accusations. In fact, for their own and their college's protection, presidents should be well-versed in the roles and tactics of the news media. An effective president will have a positive relationship with education and community beat reporters, and in cases of both newsworthy college developments and crisis management as these relationships can secure positive attention and help to avert further disaster. When the media respect and trust a president, they are far more likely to engage in cooperative and fair relationships with the college community. Knowing how to position the best message and display confidence (without appearing arrogant) are skills that can be taught and mastered. They are skills that all presidents must be taught before taking office and which will continue to be mastered throughout tenure. In short, presidents can influence what reporters cover and the messages being communicated. Unfortunately, a common mistake presidents make is that of succumbing to pressure to respond to news outlets immediately—often, before they have all the facts. This can result in collateral damage to the individuals and colleges. Presidents also need to understand when and how to employ the board chair to speak to matters of policy and institutional accountability. Going it alone is not the best policy.

Managing Student Success

As discussed in the previous chapter, community colleges recently have begun focusing more of their efforts on student success and completion. There has been a steady movement away from equating institutional success solely with enrollment growth, and toward measuring success by what is happening to students within the institution. The strategic realignment and reorganization of student support, redesign curricula, identification and use of the appropriate data matrices, incenting of student persistence, elimination of barriers, and host of other institutional imperatives require presidents to be both visionary and catalytic. More important, presidents must work closely with their boards to deepen trustee understanding of what it takes to foster student success and to develop the patience needed to evolve and sustain real change. Additionally, presidents need to cultivate skill in finessing and navigating faculty unions and the realities of collective bargaining. This means they must find ways to reinvent and encourage transformation from traditional faculty rewards and tenure systems to support systems that create and reward innovation focused on student success and completion. Reinventing institutions on student success and completion takes time, and presidents need the commitment of their boards to forge a long-term partnership that sustains real change at all levels in the institution.

LEADERSHIP FOR THE FUTURE

Higher education historically has sought to identify, groom, and advance individuals of quality to the presidency. The anticipated boom in presidential retirements suggests that higher education, and especially community colleges, needs to be more intentional in planning for presidential succession. Community-college leaders will need to redouble their efforts to cultivate the next generation of presidents. The impact of relationship building and mentoring is "the most powerful factor influencing leader trajectories are personal encouragement by respected mentors to pursue greater, senior-level positions."[13] Current presidents need to continue to reach out to senior administrators and provide encouragement to those who might be ready for the next level. And community-college boards need to foster and support such efforts. Boards need to take a more proactive approach with respect to addressing the community college leadership challenge. Boards can influence the disposition of senior administrators considering the presidency by modeling supportive and nurturing behaviors with respect to the current president, thereby advancing positive aspects of the board-president relationship.

The Role of the Board

Community college boards should ensure that the college has appropriate procedures or policies in place to assist in the identification and professional development of future leaders. Boards should monitor these procedures and policies in concert with the president to ensure their effectiveness and value to the college. For instance, do the board and president have mutually agreed-upon strategies and goals relative to identifying and preparing future leaders? The partnership between the board and president should be such that board members are respectful of the president's evaluation of senior leaders on campus who might merit mentoring or professional leadership development. Institutional rewards and incentives should be reassessed to ensure that they incent pathways to leadership that embrace vision, collaboration, and strategic alignment with institutional and community priorities.

Boards should ensure a culture of openness and candor relative to leadership development and succession planning. Time should be set aside during annual or semi-annual board retreats for this purpose. And when it comes time to search for a new president, the board should be comfortable with and knowledgeable about the presidential search process, including the appropriate constitution of a president or CEO search committee. Successful searches are guided by the principles of inclusion, honesty, and integrity with respect to candidates and the campus community. The board should strive to be cohesive and unified in its vision of the future and the traits and attributes needed in a leader. They should look to the future, not the past, when providing guidance to the search committee and/or search firm. In short, boards need to assume greater responsibility as change agents, rather than continuing to reinforce the status quo with respect to presidential leadership development. Boards have an opportunity to help redefine and reshape the college-leadership paradigm by being inquisitive and diligent in assessing and understanding trends and implications for leadership development within institutions.

Search Process

As noted earlier, the presidential or CEO search process must be deliberate, transparent, and operate with an eye focused squarely on the future. The steps for presidential searches generally involve:

1. Institutional Analysis and Profile Development;
2. Candidate Recruitment;
3. Candidate Evaluation; and
4. Selection of the New CEO[14]

The board should designate a search committee to assemble information through public meetings and forums with the board, relevant institutional profile information on the college budget and financial health, student enrollment and demographic trends, faculty composition, campus facilities and operational infrastructure, and characteristics of the community served by the institution. This information should be used to create a presidential profile that reflects the unique needs and characteristics of the college. It is imperative that important issues and institutional priorities are captured and communicated from the start. The presidential profile becomes essential in identifying and recruiting the best candidates, whose background and experience most closely mirrors the priorities and needs of the institution.

It is critically important to create support and "buy-in" from the college and the community to ensure that the presidential selection is successful and takes root within the institution. By screening candidates carefully against the college's unique profile, confidence is nurtured in campus and community stakeholders. It is incumbent upon boards to communicate the seriousness and imperative of building a climate and environment of presidential success through a process of due diligence that leads to the best decision and, ultimately, a productive long-term board/president working relationship. The board should interview candidates to ascertain overall fit with the presidential profile and needs of the institution and community. Trustees should challenge candidates to share their vision for the future and how they would move the institution forward should they be selected to run the college.

Boards hire not only institutional leaders; their choices affect the community as a whole, and their decisions can advance or undermine the compact between the college and community. Boards should invite candidates to spend time on campus to conduct both formal and informal interviews that help ensure the goals of transparency and institutional and community investiture. Thorough background and reference checks should be performed on candidates to ensure that the board has all the relevant information it needs to discharge fully its responsibilities for selecting the best and most appropriate individual to lead the institution. Boards need to adhere to the "no surprises" rule; there are few other instances during which the board's credibility will be more carefully scrutinized and reported publicly than during the presidential search and hiring process. The board must work to avoid and defuse any potential conflicts or mixed messages regarding its deliberations. The board needs to work as one body, motivated by the greater good rather than a set of competing or contradictory priorities.

The Role of President

Community college presidents should institute strategies that assist in an honest assessment of senior administrators' strengths and weakness, always with an eye toward greater leadership development. This includes allowing senior administrators opportunities to interact with and develop a deep understanding of and appreciation for the work of the governing board. Presidents should examine the internal pathways to leadership. An examination of the various means by which prospective leaders move through increasing levels of responsibility, or gain deeper understanding of the institution, should be performed regularly. Presidents should consider leadership potential when hiring senior administrators, and/or the willingness to accept or pursue increasing responsibility. Professional development opportunities, both on and off campus, should be encouraged, and adequate funds should be allocated for leadership and professional development that align with the board's goals and objectives to assure succession and leadership bench strength.

As with the board, presidents must model appropriate characteristics and leadership traits within their institutions and communities. The "do as I say, not as I do" rule undermines leadership development and succession. Presidents who are collaborative and take time to engage others in leadership build not only loyalty within the institution, but serve their boards well by deepening the leadership reserve of their institutions. Presidents should find opportunities to engage in and mentor future leaders—not only on campus, but through leadership-development programs and peer networks. Great presidents serve as ambassadors on behalf of the community college presidency. They model positive, can-do attitudes that entice others to consider becoming campus leaders, and in doing so, reap the many rewards that come with being college presidents and the satisfaction that comes with service to others.

Leadership Development Programs

Community college leadership development programs serve as an important launching ground in the recruitment and preparation of future community-college presidents. There are a multitude of college and university-based executive and higher-education leadership programs. But there are impediments that often preclude university- and college-based programs from being more influential in redefining and amplifying the presidential pipeline. These include changing institutional priorities and resources, internal competition and squabbles among academic departments and schools, and perhaps most important, general resistance to the proposition that leadership programs need to fundamentally rethink what fosters greater success in today's changing higher education landscape. Succinctly put:

> What would happen if higher education adopted a different metaphor, one more expansive; that values experiences, skills, and knowledge regardless of the positions through which individuals gained them; has multiple points of entry; and appreciated diversity?[15]

With regard to increasing leadership diversity, there are a number of leadership organizations and groups focused on specialized needs and pathways focusing greater inclusion and diversity, including the American Association for Women in Community Colleges, Kaleidoscope Leadership Institute, National Asian/Pacific Islander Council, National Community College Hispanic Council, and the National Council on Black American Affairs, just to name a few. Try as they might, however, these programs often work in isolation and are insufficient in number and resources to close the expected gap in presidential vacancies that will occur within the next ten to fifteen years. What is needed is a fundamental realignment of leadership development that is informed by what we know and see taking form on the horizon.

Confronting Realities

First, leadership-development programs need to provide real and substantive insight into today's presidential realities. What has worked well in the past no longer guarantees that individuals graduating today from leadership-development programs will be ready for the fast-paced world of the community-college presidency in the future. Programs need to be crystal clear and truly instructive about the strategic, cultural, fiscal, and operational differences that are found in today's community college environment. Creating significant mentoring programs that harness the knowledge of experienced community college presidents is important. Opportunities to shadow the president and senior administrators to learn firsthand the ins and outs of community college administration often are invaluable and cannot be substituted for by traditional classroom instruction. Future leaders must learn how to deal with multiple priorities and demands simultaneously, without becoming overwhelmed and immobilized. Specifically, future leaders should understand:

> The person needs to be "on," alert and engaged; the pace of issues, decisions, and activities is fast and relentless; and the demands of travel can exact a toll. This pace occurs day in and day out. [16]

And presidential aspirants need help in recognizing and navigating not only their own stress, but the stress often placed on their spouse, partner, and families. The president's spouse or partner often is expected and required to participate in college and community events, host receptions or dinner functions, entertain dignitaries, travel, and provide other public support. Many spouses and partners report that neither they nor their presidential counterparts had been prepared for or equipped to deal effectively with the stress of the modern college presidency. Coping skills and recognizing the effects of stress on oneself and others should be addressed in some context by leadership programs.

Changing Skill Sets

Second, leadership development programs should focus intensively on the changing skill sets necessary to succeed in today's community college. As mentioned previously, many presidents indicate that they wish that had been better prepared for the real-world challenges unique to leading a community college. Skills that enhance entrepreneurship, fundraising, crisis management, financial management, media relations, and enabling student success should be highly valued and fostered. Future leaders need to understand the importance of team-building and, more importantly, they must be able to distinguish the different types of team-building depending upon whether one is working within the institution or with business and employers, policymakers, donors, or community-based organizations. [17] While leadership most often is recognized in terms of individual qualities and success, the ability to work collaboratively and across sectors is equally important and sometimes more valuable.

Hands-on Training

Third, providing presidential aspirants with opportunities to observe and interact firsthand with a board cannot be overly emphasized. When boards search for new presidents, they look for a prospective candidate's knowledge of, and comfort with, trusteeship and trustees. It is immediately apparent to boards whether mutual respect and understanding is valued by candidates. Presidential hopefuls need to understand and support the role of the board, and in particular, the challenges faced by trustees in discharging their governance responsibilities. This extends to knowing how to interview for the presidency, résumé preparation, attire, interpersonal skills, and knowing how one's leadership style and potential is perceived by others. Leadership programs should include opportunities to observe actual community college board meetings, gain knowledge of board process and agenda setting, and talk to trustees about the partnership between boards and presidents. By understanding better the challenges faced by boards and the "human face" of trusteeship, individuals will be more successful in knowing and understanding where they best fit among the 1,200 community colleges.

FUTURE OPPORTUNITIES

While the impending presidential retirement boom is cause for concern, it is important to remember that there are hundreds, if not thousands, of potential community-college presidents working in institutions right now. As with so many challenges, opportunities abound—both for the colleges themselves and the individuals who will lead these institutions in the future. The real challenge is to redouble efforts to prepare future leaders and community-college boards to accept and embrace those future leaders. As stated previously, the process of identifying and preparing the new generation of community college presidents must be far more intentional than it has been in the past for the simple reason that presidents have more and more different responsibilities than ever before.

The emerging challenges of the twenty-first-century community college demand high-caliber visionary leaders, who are focused on the horizon of possibility, in addition to honoring the traditions and accomplishments of the past. The rewards of the community-college presidency are immense and offer real opportunities to make a difference in the lives of thousands of individuals. Each community-college president who is heralded in the news media or cited as an extraordinary leader represents only one of the incredibly talented, passionate, and committed men and women who lead community colleges today. Our challenge is to honor their service by preparing the next generation of leaders who will guide community colleges into the next century.

Chapter Seven

Moving to the Future

It is time America came to its senses. Our nation's dominant position in the world order is at great risk. We still have the capacity to lead . . . Across the globe, leaders have put their faith in education. They understand that economic growth rests largely on the quality of a nation's human resources, that national productivity depends on people's skills and educational attainment.[1]

A PARABLE FOR THE TIMES

In the blockbuster 1985 movie, *Back to the Future*,[2] a teenager named Marty McFly, alive in 1985, is sent back in time to 1955. There, Marty meets the people destined to become his parents, still in high school. By inadvertently interfering in the first meeting of his future parents, Marty mistakenly ends up as the object of his teenage mother's affections, instead of his father. Marty must find a way to set things right or risk never being born. Ultimately, Marty manages to restore historical events to their correct sequence after a series of missteps and returns "back to the future"—to his present, 1985. Marty discovers that he and his family noticeably benefit from his accidental intervention thirty years earlier. Through Marty's actions, deeds, and words, he reshapes current events and changes the future for the better—for himself, his family, and in the lives of all with whom he came into contact.

Parable Explained

The parable of traveling back in time, particularly back to the 1950s, has real resonance for understanding the growth and current plight of community colleges today. This book has attempted to explain the more pertinent reasons for that plight. The challenge that now confronts our colleges is how to propel them forward by improving their prospects through enhanced performance, leadership, and increased public investment. Allowing ourselves to revisit the past and go "back to the future" as Marty McFly was able to do, gives us a unique opportunity to remind ourselves of what worked in the past, and how those actions might be instructive for securing our present and future. When I travel throughout the United States visiting community colleges, as well as peer institutions in a number of other countries, I am struck by the vitality and energy that is embodied in and emanating from those institutions. That vitality and energy is the living legacy of the policies, investments, commitment, and "can do" attitude of all that came before. Marty's experience, while admittedly only the stuff of Hollywood, makes me reflect on how the past shapes the future, and that by understanding our past, the journey forward becomes more clearly illuminated. It is with this parable in mind that I search for answers, while gathering the resolve to strengthen our colleges and elevate them to ever-higher prominence and esteem.

Revisiting the Past

Harvard University economists Claudia Goldin and Lawrence F. Katz tell the story of American education and its impact on the evolution of contemporary society and culture in their book, *The Race Between Education and Technology*, released in 2008. Through rigorous economic and policy analysis, they retrace decisions made by government to foster and support public education. Specifically, Goldin and Katz chronicle the history behind extending education universally throughout our society and the deep impact of that history on the present. They argue that the intentionality with which we as a society invested in education, including community colleges, thrust America into its undisputed role of world economic and innovation leader.

By embracing the principles of access and equality, the nation was able to capitalize on expanding intellectual capital fueled by the Baby Boom generation. Dual forces of rising educational attainment through higher education and rapid fire technological innovation fueled huge gains in productivity that rippled through our economic system. America was catapulted to the position of world leader, enjoying one of the longest and most pervasive periods of economic expansion than in any other time in the nation's past. Income inequality was reduced, home ownership exploded, and the American Dream became an affordable currency of the time and a reality for millions of individuals.

Yet something derailed America's educational gains, which began to wane in the last quarter of the twentieth century:

> Educational attainment, as measured by the completed schooling levels of successive cohorts, was exceptionally rapid and continuous for the first three-quarters of the twentieth century. But the educational advance slowed consid-

erably for young adults beginning in the 1970s and for the overall labor force by the early 1980s. For cohorts born from the 1870s to about 1950, every decade was accompanied by an increase of about 0.8 years of education. During that 80-year period the vast majority of parents had children whose educational attainment greatly exceeded theirs. Educational change between the generations then came to an abrupt standstill. An important part of the American dream, that children will do better than their parents, was threatened.[3]

Why did wheels on the bus of progress come undone in the mid-1970s? Goldin and Katz attribute the turn-around in educational attainment to eroding public investment in education, and an apparent relaxation of the values of rigor, hard work, and persistence, which had previously combined to drive up educational attainment rates. In support of our parable of revisiting the past to ensure the future, Goldin and Katz conclude their book with the chilling exhortation that we, as a nation, seemingly have forgotten our own past—that is, the collective actions that we as a society undertook to secure the future. They conclude their book by imploring that we "shed our collective amnesia."[4] I agree. I believe that if we don't shed our amnesia, we won't be able to rejoin Marty McFly in the future.

THINKING BIG, ACTING BOLDLY

The clear and present danger confronting the United States today, to quote American philosopher and poet George Santayana, is that "those who cannot remember the past are condemned to repeat it."[5] Given the many challenges of the new millennium, retracing our steps and remembering what worked in the past provides invaluable guidance for how to correct and avoid missteps in the future. It also provides useful insight into reshaping the future by unleashing the power of community colleges to help put the wheels back on the bus. At the end of World War II, America's leaders embraced big picture thinking and took bold actions to secure the future.

Preparing for Employment

On June 22, 1944, President Franklin D. Roosevelt signed into law the Servicemen's Readjustment Act, or GI Bill of Rights as it came to be known. The GI Bill of Rights represented the largest national education and training investment of its time. The impetus behind Congressional support was the need to curtail the near certainty of imminent mass unemployment, as more than 15 million servicemen returned from the military theaters of war to day-to-day lives requiring vastly different skills. Having emerged from the Great

Depression only a decade earlier, Congress and the administration mobilized through the GI Bill of Rights to ensure that economic history would not be repeated.

The funds disbursed to veterans were significant over the ten-year period following the end of the Second World War. The legislation effectively blunted the impact of near-certain unemployment as millions of able-bodied men and women returned from the European and Pacific theaters of war. It helped turn the prospect of economic collapse into unprecedented economic growth and opportunity. Once the GI Bill of Rights was enacted:

> Within the following 7 years, approximately 8 million veterans received educational benefits. Under the act, approximately 2,300,000 attended colleges and universities, 3,500,000 received school training, and 3,400,000 received on-the-job training. The number of degrees awarded by U.S. colleges and universities more than doubled between 1940 and 1950, and the percentage of Americans with bachelor degrees, or advanced degrees, rose from 4.6 percent in 1945 to 25 percent a half-century later.
>
> By 1956, when it expired, the education-and-training portion of the GI Bill had disbursed $14.5 billion to veterans—but the Veterans Administration estimated the increase in Federal income taxes alone would pay for the cost of the bill several times over.[6]

Initially, the GI Bill of Rights propelled some 1.7 million veterans to enroll in higher education, accounting for 71 percent of students enrolled in colleges and universities.[7] The most important legacy it created, however, was the hundreds of thousands of newly credentialed professionals flooding the labor force. Historian Milton Greenberg, who has written widely about the impact of the GI Bill of Rights and of veterans-benefit programs, succinctly described the impact on the labor force:

> By the time the initial GI Bill eligibility for World War II veterans expired in 1956—about 11 years after final victory—the United States was richer by 450,000 trained engineers, 240,000 accountants, 238,000 teachers, 91,000 scientists, 67,000 doctors, 22,000 dentists, and more than a million other college-educated individuals.[8]

The GI Bill of Rights represented a significant financial commitment by the United States at the time. In 1944, the national gross domestic product (GDP) was $219.8 billion.[9] At the time of its enactment, the GI Bill of Rights constituted an investment of roughly 6.5 percent of total 1944 GDP. By comparison with today, U.S. gross domestic product at the close of 2011 equaled $15.3 trillion,[10] nearly 70 times greater in current dollars than in 1944. Converting the $14.5 billion from 1944 dollars to current 2011 dollars, the same GI Bill of Rights would represent an investment of some $182 billion today.[11] It has been estimated that the United States spent $122 billion in 2011 fighting the Taliban insurgency in Afghanistan, [12] while the post 9/11 GI Bill enacted in 2008 provided $63 billion over ten years for veterans' education and training. [13] As noted, the impact of the GI Bill of Rights on the American economy was vast and continues paying dividends today. Parenthetically, my own father was a beneficiary of the GI Bill of Rights, and he later joined the ranks of academe as a scientist, researcher, and professor. The GI Bill of Rights constituted a bold and innovative initiative that fueled the democratization of higher education—a powerful example of investment the nation once committed, and one which economists Goldin and Katz argue made the United States a dominant force after World War II. An educated citizenry is fundamental to our democracy. Thomas Jefferson opined in his letter to George Wythe in 1789 that education was the foundation for "the preservation of freedom and happiness." [14] So important is this notion, government has struggled to promote and foster its acceptance and establishment for as long as we have had a Republic.

Expanding the Network

While the GI Bill of Rights primarily represented an economic and employment strategy, it was clear that the nation needed to embark on yet another voyage to serve the rapidly expanding U.S. population and maintain an economy that was capable of producing new public investment opportunities. In 1947, President Harry S. Truman convened the President's Commission on Higher Education—a group of luminaries and scholars—whose charge was:

> defining the responsibilities of colleges and universities in American democracy and in international affairs—and, more specifically, with reexamining the objectives, methods, and facilities of higher education in the United States in the light of the social role it has to play. [15]

Among the Commission's recommendations was that the nation embark on a deliberate strategy to broaden access to public education beyond high school, to create a K–14 educational system that should be both universal and free. This recommendation, more than any other of its kind, fueled the construction and spread of community colleges across the national landscape. The Truman Commission, like the GI Bill of Rights, enlarged our notions of access and fueled the imagination as to the benefits of public higher education for a broad segment of the population. As noted earlier, the number of community colleges more than quadrupled, and as a result, a robust network of public colleges was franchised in virtually every community.

STEM

On October 4, 1957, the nation was abruptly shaken by the sobering reality that the then Soviet Union had beaten the United States into space. The successful deployment of Sputnik rocked the political establishment and highlighted America's need to invest in the fields of science, technology, engineering, and mathematics—the so-called STEM fields as they are known today. Congress responded by passing the National Defense Education Act (NDEA), which President Dwight D. Eisenhower signed on September 2, 1958. NDEA authorized a massive investment in STEM curricula and student access—a billion dollars—to ensure that America's youth would become leading innovators of the future. NDEA also provided financial assistance to increase the number of students pursuing STEM fields. While difficult to precisely quantify, analysis of the impact of NDEA showed that it produced positive results in the:

> [. . .] rate of high school, college, and graduate completion; in the level of student preparedness in science, mathematics . . . ; in the number of teachers and degree-granting institutions; in the number of bachelors and doctoral degrees awarded; and in the number of scholarly publications by doctoral recipients.[16]

Three years after NDEA was passed, in 1961, President John F. Kennedy challenged the nation during his address to a Joint Session of Congress by saying, "I believe that this nation should commit itself to achieving the goal, before this decade is out, of landing a man on the moon and returning him safely to the Earth."[17] Astronaut Neil Armstrong's unforgettable first step onto the surface of the Moon on July 20, 1969 would not have been possible without the contribution made by NDEA to increase the number STEM graduates, some of whom later went on to become NASA scientists and engineers.

Delivering on the Dream

Thrust into the presidency by the tragic events that occurred in Dallas, Texas on November 22, 1963, President Lyndon B. Johnson used his formidable legislative and political skills to set about creating the "Great Society." One of the bills signed into law by Johnson—The Civil Rights Act of 1964—constituted a sea change legislation for the social fabric of the United States. The act made discrimination against African Americans and women, as well as the practice of racial segregation, illegal throughout the nation. The act also ended racial segregation in schools and in other public sector organizations—work that began under the landmark Supreme Court decision of Brown v. Board of Education of Topeka, 347 U.S. 483, in 1954. The Civil

Rights Act of 1964 instituted a systematic "democratization" of America's public institutions, and helped to realize the "dream" eloquently described by Reverend Martin Luther King, Jr. the year before on the steps of the Lincoln Memorial.

In addition to the Civil Rights Act of 1964, Johnson also signed the Higher Education Act (HEA) of 1965. It has been noted that:

> The main impetus for the Higher Education Act was President Johnson's desire to use education as a tool for economic growth and development, an approach that fit within his broader social policy agenda. [18]

The HEA expanded the federal role in college access that was initiated through the GI Bill of Rights, serving to advance the twin goals of increasing educational attainment and fostering opportunity. In addition to providing federal funds to colleges and universities for strengthening educational programs, the HEA created federal student-loan and scholarship programs, as well as a teacher corps initiative. Today, federal student-assistance programs comprise a \$157 billion[19] annual commitment to student postsecondary education access, including community colleges.

COMMUNITY COLLEGES: A BIG IDEA

Thinking big and investing for success represent quintessential American values. Other nations are ramping up their investment in access and the educational attainment of people, challenging the United States' competitive advantage. In the 2005 bestseller *The World is Flat*, *New York Times* journalist Thomas Friedman argued that education's role in nurturing innovation in nations like China and India contributed to flattening the world economy, thereby leveling the playing field between nations. Friedman, like many these days, has become a proponent of the nation's community colleges as catalysts for bolstering education and innovation:

> While expanding research universities on the high end of the spectrum is important, so is expanding the availability of technical schools and community colleges. Everyone should have a chance to be educated beyond high school. Otherwise upper-income kids will get those skills and their slice, and the lower-income kids will never get a chance. We have to increase the government subsidies that make it possible for more and more kids to attend community colleges and more and more low-skilled workers to get retrained. JFK wanted to put a man on the moon. My vision is to put every American man or woman on a campus. [20]

In the same way that President Johnson's Civil Rights Act made Martin Luther King, Jr.'s vision a reality, community colleges are the big idea necessary to make Friedman's dream a reality. Other nations have begun to realize this and are scrambling to create their own community college systems. The community college model was developed in the United States, and for most of the past century, the United States alone claimed virtually all of the community and technical colleges on the planet. If imitation is the "sincerest form of flattery" to paraphrase Charles Caleb Colton,[21] the American community college system has many admirers across the globe eager to replicate in some way what we often take for granted. Neighboring nations of Canada and Mexico have community colleges, as do other nations throughout the world—including those I have visited—Belize, Denmark, Jordan, Saudi Arabia, and the United Kingdom. As America's universities are the modern descendants of the great European universities, our community colleges have spawned progeny across the globe, enabling countries to democratize their higher education systems to fuel their own economic and human capital development.

Friedman's vision also serves as the "back to the future" parable in action. It connects past policies and investments to possibilities of the future and continued national progress. More importantly, it succinctly advocates for the power of community colleges to increase educational attainment, thereby reducing income inequality by allowing more Americans to access real economic opportunity. Friedman is not alone in his admiration of community colleges, or in understanding their critical role in securing our future. Longtime U.S. Federal Reserve Board of Governors Chairman Allan Greenspan observed in a speech at Boston College in Massachusetts in 2004:

> One area in which educational investments appear to have paid off is our community colleges . . . These two-year institutions are playing a similar role in preparing our students for work life as did our early twentieth-century high schools in that less technically oriented era. But to an even greater extent, our population today is adjusting to an ever-faster turnover of jobs. We are also growing more aware that in the current intensely competitive economy, the pace of job creation and destruction implies that the average work life will span many jobs and even more than one profession. . . . America's reputation as the world's leader in higher education is grounded in the ability of these versatile institutions to serve the practical needs of the economy by teaching and training and, more significantly, by unleashing the creative thinking that moves our economy forward.[22]

Greenspan's comments were a reminder of the necessity of recognizing and supporting community colleges as an economic and workforce engine. David Wessel, author and *Wall Street Journal* reporter, reflecting on the need to increase respect and understanding of community colleges, commented on the forthcoming White House Summit on Community Colleges in 2010 in this fashion:

> Community colleges get their few moments in the White House limelight next week when President Barack Obama and the vice president's wife, Jill Biden, convene a community-college summit. It's another step toward giving the institutions, the Rodney Dangerfields of higher education, a bit more of the respect they deserve.[23]

Truthfully, many kudos have been bestowed on community colleges in recent years, and the attention is welcomed and well-deserved. But praise ultimately rings hollow without the investment of real resources and a sustained strategy for freeing the immense potential of community colleges to restore the momentum and progress of the past.

Early in 2004, before Greenspan spoke in Boston about community colleges, President George W. Bush invoked the necessity of supporting the nation's community colleges during his State of the Union Address to a Joint Session of Congress. Mentioning community colleges specifically in a State of the Union address for the first time ever, President Bush stated:

> I propose increasing our support for America's fine community colleges, so they can . . . train workers for industries that are creating the most new jobs.[24]

Following the State of the Union address, the Bush administration unveiled the Community-Based Job Training Grants (CBJTG) program, initially funded by Congress at $125 million to support community college efforts to prepare individuals for high-demand, high-skill jobs. In its first year, the CBJTG program supported twenty-one community-college programs.

While the program was eliminated in 2010, another program essentially took its place. The Trade Adjustment Assistance Community College and Career Training (TAACCCT) Grant Program was created through the Health Care and Education Reconciliation Act (HCERA) and signed by President Barack Obama on March 30, 2010, on a campus of Northern Virginia Community College. The HCERA included $2 billion over four years to fund the TAACCCT program. As described on the U.S. Department of Labor website:

> TAACCCT provides community colleges and other eligible institutions of higher education with funds to expand and improve their ability to deliver education and career training programs that can be completed in two years or less, are suited for workers who are eligible for training under the TAA for Workers program, and prepare program participants for employment in high-wage, high-skill occupations. Through these multi-year grants, the Department of Labor is helping to ensure that our nation's institutions of higher education are helping adults succeed in acquiring the skills, degrees, and credentials

needed for high-wage, high-skill employment while also meeting the needs of employers for skilled workers. The Department is implementing the TAACCCT program in partnership with the Department of Education. [25]

The first round of TAACCCT awards were announced in autumn 2011, with nearly $500 million going to community colleges to support partnerships with employers focusing on preparing Americans for gainful employment in a rapidly changing labor market. This investment, while welcomed, cannot replace or supplant the erosion of public funds for community colleges over the past few decades. What is needed are new and bold initiatives to reconnect and re-engage community colleges for the heavy lifting needed to restore the nation's workforce and economic systems to robust health.

ACTIONS, NOT WORDS

From 1988 to present, community colleges have attempted repeatedly to rally the nation to action by highlighting their role and importance. A 1988 report, *Building Communities: A Vision for a New Century*, argued that community colleges have represented "good stewards of the public dollar."[26] In recognition of their stewardship, the report urged states to strengthen public financing for community colleges and revamp funding formulas to align more closely with the services provided to students. Building off the 1988 report, the American Association of Community Colleges and Association of Community College Trustees, with support from the W. K. Kellogg Foundation, issued *The Knowledge Net* in 2000. Contemporizing the issues confronting community colleges on the advent of the new millennium, the report sought to focus attention on the struggle of institutions in meeting growing demands with stagnate funding streams. The report urged community college leaders to leverage increased public funding:

> By using a strategic approach and seeking political allies who share common goals, community colleges must aggressively make their case for greater funding to accommodate increased enrollment and service needs. [27]

And more recently in 2008, the College Board's National Commission on Community Colleges issued a report recommending a landmark piece of national legislation to resource and connect community colleges more closely to the nation's workforce development needs by urging that:

> Congress and the President cooperate to enact the Community College Competitiveness Act: federal legislation that will bring community colleges fully into the twenty-first century and allow them to respond to the challenges facing the nation's workforce. [28]

The College Board's recommendation was a big idea—an idea that is worthy of the nation's efforts to rebuild economic and labor force capacity. Tragically, it, along with many other worthy ideas, has yet to transition from words to actions. So how are we to move from inactive words to actions that will fully engage community colleges as change agents and more fully integrate them into our education and work force systems? Community colleges cannot go it alone. They must be joined by government and society, as a whole, with each playing specific roles if we are to reach a future of promise and progress.

Community Colleges

Community colleges owe their legacy to virtues and ideals of our democracy. As such, they have a responsibility not only to maintain this legacy, but to work to ensure that the legacy remains firmly planted and nurtured for the benefit of future generations. We need to respect the past, but to think differently about the future.

Embrace a Culture of Evidence

Community college leaders must assume greater responsibility for the outcomes—positive and negative—generated by their institutions. They must find ways to increase educational attainment rates across the broad spectrum of student populations. Completion must be defined in ways that honor and embrace institutional mission and goals and the aspirations of students. Community college governing boards, presidents, administrators, and faculty must be more intentional in analyzing and measuring the impact of the programs and services they provide. They should set goals and performance targets that are ambitious enough to foster change, but which are also attainable.

Adopt the Right Matrices

Community colleges must embrace the need to develop and apply new measures that more closely align to their mission and the populations they serve. Using anecdotal information, while emotionally compelling, will not convince policymakers to increase investment in community colleges. Using the right matrices, and squarely facing the music of intense scrutiny, will help convince government of institutional commitment to improvement. The commitment to improve could bring with it enhanced flexibility and autonomy for the dollars government provides.

Communicate Results

Moral courage is needed to confront infrastructure that is not working well and to make the necessary corrections. Data on student success and completion relative to institutional mission should be transparent and communicated broadly, both within the institution and with external stakeholders. Students, parents, policymakers, and others should not have to search for data that speak to program effectiveness and student success. The data should be readily available through the college website and other media, just like the course catalogue.

Minding the Front Door

Community colleges should pay far more attention to orienting students and preparing them to navigate successfully through their institutions. Allowing students the "right to fail" should no longer be an option. Community colleges should redouble efforts to assess, advise, and mentor students about their educational goals and aspirations. More should be done to understand the reasons why students leave without completing what they start. And community colleges should focus more intensively on strategies that eliminate barriers to persistence and completion. Community colleges need to exploit new media—particularly social media—to create virtual communities of learners, tightly connected to and engaged with institutions.

Boards

Community college boards need to embrace continuous education and trustee development programs to achieve higher levels of effectiveness if they are to be strong partners in helping colleges navigate the chasm between demand and resources. Progress and effectiveness should be evaluated through ongoing self-assessment that aids in building shared goals among board members. Boards should direct institutional leaders to ensure that academic and business models are capable of exploiting new and emerging resource opportunities, while at the same time, eliminating programs and services with diminishing returns. As public stewards, trustees should intensify their advocacy efforts on behalf of their institutions and communities, serving as a voice of reason in the allocation of public resources.

Leadership/Faculty Development

A much greater sense of urgency and deliberateness is needed to identify and prepare new talent for leadership in community colleges. Leadership development and recruitment should place a high premium on cultivating and nurturing vision, adeptness at managing and prioritizing multiple demands simultaneously, coalition and team building, advocacy, finance and resources management, media savvy, and managing change and student success. Faculty development should be encouraged, particularly new methods and pedagogy that foster greater student success and achievement.

Government

Government—local, state, and federal—needs to step up to the plate as it has done in past periods of our history. The compact between public investment and community colleges is languishing, and the responsibility for maintaining community colleges is being shifted increasingly to students, who are least able to afford college. Nowhere is this clearer than in the current state of student financial assistance.

Assisting Students

Where grants once were valued to promote access to higher education, student loans, particularly in the private-loan market, have begun to take precedence. The nation faces yet another debt crisis similar to the home mortgage crisis that helped precipitate the last economic recession: student-loan debt is already estimated to exceed $1 trillion.[29] Student-loan debt represents a crippling burden on college students and it limits choices among professional and occupational fields to those whose income is sufficient to allow repaying debt. Community-college tuition is significantly lower than that of four-year colleges and universities, and technical job-training programs, which are still affordable, move individuals into needed skilled-labor jobs. Community colleges aren't just economically important because they are more affordable, but also because they diversify skills, foster greater balance between jobs created and skills needed, and contribute to needed social-labor services like health care and first responders. If left unaddressed, student loan debt will corrode the nation's need to increase educational attainment.

Renew the Compact

We need to revitalize the compact between government and community colleges. If community colleges are such "good stewards of the public dollar," as characterized by the *Building Communities* report, they should be rewarded with greater investment so they can produce human capital for the nation. Regulation and government oversight should incentivize results and relevance to economic and social imperatives—not brandish the stick as the first resort. Government at all levels must renew its compact with community colleges that deliver programs and services the public needs and support them financially. We must resist further slippage in governmental funding formulas or statutorily mandated funding streams by demanding that government and policymakers be equally accountable in what they give to us as they demand in return.

Reward Performance

Government should support and subscribe to community college efforts to create voluntary systems of accountability that embrace and empower innovation. It is important that agencies of state and federal government respect and understand the importance of self-tailoring assessment and performance outcomes to institutional mission. "One size fits all" approaches do irreparable harm to institutions—particularly to community colleges—further impeding progress toward increased educational attainment. College leaders and boards should be charged with accurately and precisely assessing community college outcomes. The Voluntary Framework of Accountability discussed earlier in the book will give community college boards and presidents the ammunition they need to convince government to work in partnership with accountability—not in opposition by maintaining or creating systems that mismatch outcomes to institutional mission.

Society

Goldin and Katz remind us that we must find a way back to embracing the values of rigor and persistence that worked well in the past. We have become too accustomed to instant gratification, of endlessly substituting "wants" in place of "needs." Whereas America once was the "land of milk and honey" we have allowed ourselves to become the "land of milk and plastic"—credit cards have become the financiers of our dreams. Because so much capital has been directed to short-term consumption, we have been negligent in our investment in the long-term—institutions that generate economic output and create meaningful jobs for future generations. Society must re-embrace the essential partnership that exists between colleges and community. All of us must eschew the fallacy that we can continue to receive more by paying less.

EMBRACING THE PARABLE

Investing in community colleges has been a big part of American prosperity since the end of World War II. Regaining our position of global leadership by increasing educational attainment rates is the way out of our current economic malaise. Imagine what might happen if 1,200 community colleges, supported through enhanced investment, each made the necessary effort to increase educational attainment over the remainder of this decade. The math is not too difficult—5 million more degrees by 1,200 colleges by 2020—something to fuel the imagination.

Competition

We face many challenges, but none as great as increased competition from overseas, and especially from those countries that are investing more in education and using new technologies to realign educational entities as a means for increasing educational attainment rates and exploiting emerging economic opportunities. If other countries understand the nexus between education and economic prowess, and are willing to invest more as a proportion of their wealth, America's future will be both challenging and uncertain. In the years that I have been privileged to work in support of community colleges and their governing boards, I have experienced the sights, sounds, and sensations of an incredibly dynamic and powerful enterprise that is reshaping America's landscape. Community colleges are the unheralded institutions of our democracy. This must change, and change soon.

Seeing is Believing

The things that I have seen in my travels convince me that community colleges constitute game changers. In Flint, Michigan, I saw a vibrant learning center in the heart of a community long since devastated by the decline of the American auto industry. Because of a community college, Flint endures. I spoke with students enrolled in community colleges in the New York City metropolitan area. Because of those institutions, students who previously knew only failure and disappointment are in school training for real occupations that are in demand. They have a renewed sense of dignity and purpose. I recall listening to a student in North Carolina who left his community college program short of completion—a failure by conventional norms. He landed a job with a manufacturing company, and within two years, was earning more than the president of the community college from which he acquired his training. I sat in an airport eavesdropping on a mother-daughter conversation in which the daughter was articulately and effectively convincing her mother that the community college was a better alternative for her than a four-year college. "I'll get better instruction," she said, and "at half the price." How can you argue with that?

Ingenuity and Innovation

Investment in higher education for all citizens—all of them—made our country a dominant economic and military power throughout the latter half of the twentieth century. We know empirically and historically that education matters; that expanding access is the accelerator to progress and greater shared prosperity:

> No institution better reflects American ingenuity and innovation than community colleges. Uniquely American, our 1,200 community colleges serve virtually every community in the nation, enroll almost half of all U.S. undergraduates and power economic activity that changes lives and communities everyday.[30]

Community colleges represent dynamic and exciting institutions. Almost without exception, trustees, presidents, administrators, faculty, and operations personnel believe in their institutions and work hard to ensure their success. Community college leadership requires the blending of common sense with the ability to inspire, to see what others miss, and to orchestrate partnerships and relationships that serve to magnify the impact beyond what only a handful of people might achieve. While many challenges lie ahead, there is cause for optimism as long as community colleges remain on the scene. Their legacy of innovation, flexibility, and responsiveness undergirds our democracy and carries the nutrients of access and opportunity to all parts of the population. When I think about the challenges we face, I recall the words of President Clinton during his first Presidential Inaugural Address on January 20, 1993:

> There is nothing wrong with America that cannot be cured by what is right with America.[31]

Community colleges are "what is right with America." The rest is up to us.

Notes

TOMORROW'S CHALLENGES TODAY

1. Giuseppe Tomasi di Lampedusa. *Il Gattopardo* (Milano, Italy: Casa editrice Feltrinelli, 1958).

2. J. Noah Brown. "The Road Ahead," *Trustee Quarterly* (Fall 2011): pp. 10-11.

3. See www.aacc.nche.edu/AboutCC/whsummit/Documents/boggs_whsummitbrief.pdf.

4. Reference by Mary Ellen Duncan, former president of Howard Community College in Maryland. She referred to the two-year institution as the "Ellis Island" of higher education in "The State of American Higher Education: What Are Parents, Students, and Taxpayers Getting for Their Money?" as part of a Statement of the American Association of Community Colleges to the U.S. House of Representatives Committee on Education and the Workforce, May 2003.

5. The term is frequently used throughout community college promotional materials at dozens of community colleges.

6. *2011 Community College Fast Facts* (Washington, DC: American Association of Community Colleges, 2011).

7. Ibid.

8. Ibid.

9. Ibid.

10. See www.communitycollegetimes.com/Pages/Campus-Issues/cc-enrollments.aspx.

11. See http://economix.blogs.nytimes.com/2010/04/28/college-enrollment-rate-at-record-high/.

12. "Engines of Prosperity." Fact sheet prepared by the Association of Community College Trustees and Economic Modeling Specialists, Inc., Washington, DC, 2007.

13. Ibid.

14. See www.whitehouse.gov/communitycollege.

15. The inequitable funding situation of community colleges is discussed in more detail in chapter 4.

16. While there is some debate over the true origin of this quotation, it is most frequently attributed to German-born U.S. physicist Albert Einstein (1879–1955).

17. Additional consequences from an increasing dependence on adjunct faculty will be explored in chapter 6.

18. Terry O'Banion. *The Rogue Trustee: The Elephant in the Room* (Phoenix, AZ: League for Innovation in the Community College, 2008).

19. Doug Lederman. "State Funds for Higher Education Fell by 7.6% in 2011–12." Inside Higher Ed, January 23, 2012. www.insidehighered.com/news/2012/01/23/state-funds-higher-education-fell-76-2011-12.

20. Ibid.

21. Elizabeth McNichol, Phil Oliff and Nicholas Johnson. "States Continue to Fell Recession's Impact." Center on Budget and Policy Priorities, February 27, 2012, p. 1. www.cbpp.org/cms/index.cfm?fa=view&id=711.

22. Ibid.

LEADING WITH ACCOUNTABILITY

1. *The American Heritage® Dictionary of the English Language*, fourth edition (Boston: Houghton Mifflin Company, 2009).

2. U.S. Department of Education. *Digest of Education Statistics, 2010* (NCES 2011-015) (Washington, DC: U.S. Government Printing Office), table 5.

3. See http://nces.ed.gov/programs/digest/d10/tables/dt10_244.asp.

4. See www.nytimes.com/2011/08/22/opinion/the-hidden-costs-of-higher-ed.html.

5. Paul Bradley. "Get Results, Get Paid," *Community College Week*, February 20, 2012, p. 7. www.ccweek.com/news/templates/template.aspx?articleid=2938&zoneid=7.

6. Kevin J. Dougherty. "State Performance Funding for Higher Education—Impacts, Stability, Demise: Policy Lessons." Presentation to the National Conference of State Legislatures, March 13, 2010.

7. U.S. Supreme Court Justice Potter Stewart, concurring opinion in *Jacobellis v. Ohio* 378 U.S. 184 (1964), which pointed to the overall difficulty in devising one national or common standard relating to indecency.

8. The author developed this cautionary list in speeches before community college audiences on the need for a more informed and proactive discussion of community college accountability matrices.

9. J. Noah Brown. "Standards that Fit: Community Colleges Aim to Create a New Accountability System," *CASE Currents* (January 2010): 11.

10. See www.fldoe.org/cc/students/bach_degree.asp.

11. See www.accbd.org/resources/baccalaureate-conferring-locations/?ct=US.

12. *2011 Community College Fast Facts* (Washington, DC: American Association of Community Colleges, 2011).

13. S. Aud, W. Hussar, G. Kena, K. Bianco, L. Frohlich, J. Kemp, and K. Tahan. *The Condition of Education, 2011* (NCES 2011-033). (Washington, DC: U.S. Government Printing Office, 2011), 71.

14. Kevin J. Dougherty, Rachel Hare Bork, and Rebecca S. Natow. "Performance Accountability Systems for Community Colleges: Lessons for the Voluntary Framework of Accountability for Community Colleges," Community College Research Center, November 2, 2009, p. i. http:// http://ccrc.tc.columbia.edu/Publication.asp?UID=728.

15. Ibid.

16. Ibid.

17. Gail O. Mellow and Cynthia Heelan. *Minding the Dream: The Process and Practice of the American Community College* (Lanham, MD: Rowman & Littlefield, 2008), 51–52

18. Center for Community College Engagement. *A Matter of Degrees: Promising Practices for Community College Student Success* (Austin: The University of Texas–Austin, 2012), 6. http:// www.ccsse.org/center/resources/docs/publications/a_Matter_of_degrees_02-02-12.pdf.

19. Ibid.

20. "Winning the Skills Race and Strengthening America's Middle Class: An Action Agenda for Community Colleges," *The Report of The National Commission on Community Colleges* (January 2008): 9.

21. "Why VFA?" American Association of Community Colleges. See www.aacc.nche.edu/Resources/aaccprograms/vfa/Pages/WhyVFA.aspx.

22. Ibid.

23. Ibid.

24. Ibid.

25. "Voluntary Framework of Accountability: Current Status." American Association of Community Colleges. See www.aacc.nche.edu/Resources/aaccprograms/VFAWeb/Pages/VFAStatus.aspx

26. "Why VFA?" American Association of Community Colleges. See www.aacc.nche.edu/Resources/aaccprograms/vfa/Pages/WhyVFA.aspx.

27. www.learningoutcomeassessment.org/AboutUs.html.

CITIZEN GOVERNANCE

1. The Merriam-Webster Unabridged Dictionary. www.merriam-webster.com/dictionary/trustee.

2. The Morrill Act of 1862 established the nation's network of land-grant colleges and universities, followed later by the Smith Lever Act of 1914, which created the "cooperative extension," further expanding the reach of land-grant colleges and universities to the nation's agricultural sector.

3. *Higher Education for Democracy: A Report of the President's Commission on Higher Education*, Volume 1: Establishing the Goals (New York: Harper and Brothers, 1947), 32–39.

4. See www.aacc.nche.edu/AboutCC/history/Pages/ccgrowth.aspx.

5. Cindra J. Smith. *Trusteeship in Community Colleges: A Guide for Effective Governance* (Washington, DC: Association of Community College Trustees, 2000), 2.

6. "State Governance and Community Colleges" (Denver, CO: Education Commission of the States, 1998), table III.

7. Information from the Minnesota Office of Higher Education, http://www.ohe.state.mn.us/.

8. Community College trustees in California receive stipends in exchange for their service as authorized through state statute.

9. Association of Community College Trustees. *The Citizen Trustee: Profile in Leadership*, March 2010, p. 1. www.acct.org/Citizen%20Trustee%20Initial%20Findings.pdf.

10. Ibid., 2.

11. Ibid., 2.

12. Ibid., 2.

13. Ibid., 2.

14. Ibid., 2.

15. Ibid., 3.

16. Ibid., 3.

17. Ibid., 4.

18. Ibid., 4.

19. Ibid., 4.

20. Ibid., 4.

21. Ibid., 1.

22. Ibid., 4.

23. Ibid., 4.

24. *2011 AGB Survey of Higher Education Governance*. Association of Governing Boards of Universities and Colleges, 2011, p. 1. http://agb.org/reports/2011/2011-agb-survey-higher-education-governance.

25. "Guide to Trustee Roles and Responsibilities." Association of Community College Trustees. www.acct.org/resources/center/roles-responsibilities.php.

26. See www.mdc.edu/main/about/mission_vision.asp.

27. Gail O. Mellow and Cynthia Heelan. *Minding the Dream: The Process and Practice of the American Community College* (Lanham, MD: Rowman & Littlefield, 2008), 77.

28. Ibid.

29. Ibid.

30. Ibid.

31. Ibid.

32. Much more around data analysis and disaggregation is found in chapter 5.

33. Ibid.

34. North Carolina General Statutes, Article 1—General Provisions for State Administration.(1963, c. 448, s. 23; 1979, c. 462, s. 2; c. 896, s. 13; 1979, 2nd Sess., c. 1130, s. 1; 1989, c. 521, s. 2; 1995, c. 470, s. 2.).

35. Arkansas Code Annotated, Title 6, Education, Subtitle 5. Postsecondary and Higher Education Generally, Chapter 61 Postsecondary Institutions Generally, Subchapter 2—Arkansas Higher Education Coordinating Board, § 6-61-202 (2011).

36. West Virginia Code § 18B-1D-9.

37. See www.acct.org/membership/state/state-listing.php.

38. "The Case for Effective State-level Education Programs for Public College and University Trustees." Association of Governing Boards of Universities and Colleges, July 2004, p. 1. http://agb.org/reports/2004/case-effective-state-level-education-programs-public-college-and-university-trustees-0.

39. "Standard IV: Leadership and Governance." Accrediting Commission for Community and Junior Colleges, Western Association of Schools and Colleges, Sacramento, CA, adopted June 2002, p. 25. http://www.accjc.org/wp-content/uploads/2010/09/Accreditation-Standards-Annotated-for-CQI-and-SLOs_Revised-June-20122.pdf.

40. "Standards for Accreditation," Standard 3.4, Organization and Governance. New England Association of Schools and Colleges, Commission on Institutions of Higher Education, Bedford, MA, July 1, 2011. http://cihe.neasc.org/standards_policies/standards/.

41. "Guide to Appointing and Electing Community College Trustees." Association of Community College Trustees. http://www.acct.org/resources/center/guide-to-electing-and-appointi.php.

RESOURCES AND SCARCITY

1. *Building Communities: A Vision for a New Century. A Report of the Commission of the Future of Community Colleges* (Washington, DC: American Association of Community and Junior Colleges, 1988), 45.

2. Center on Budget and Policy Priorities. *Survey of the States* (Washington, DC: Center on Budget and Policy Priorities, 2010).

3. *State Higher Education Finance, FY 2010.* (Boulder, CO: State Higher Education Executive Officers, 2011), 7.

4. Nicholas Johnson, Phil Oliff, and Erica Williams. *An Update on State Budget Cuts.* Center on Budget and Policy Priorities, February 2011, p. 11. www.cbpp.org/cms/index.cfm?fa=view&id=1214

5. Ibid., 11–12.

6. See www.aacc.nche.edu/AboutCC/Trends/Pages/publiccommunitycollegerevenueby-source.aspx.

7. Ibid.

8. See www.nber.org/cycles.html.

9. Christopher M. Mullin. "Doing More with Less: The Inequitable Funding of Community Colleges" (Washington, DC: American Association of Community Colleges, September 2010), 5, figure 1.

10. Ibid., 10.

11. Ibid., 10.

12. Charles N. Earl. Foreword to *Uncertain Recovery: Access and Funding Issues in Public Higher Education. Findings from the 2010 Survey of the National Council of State Directors of Community Colleges* (Tuscaloosa, AL: University of Alabama Education Policy Center, 2010), v.

13. Christopher M. Mullen. *Doing More with Less: The Inequitable Funding of Community Colleges*. American Association of Community Colleges, Policy Brief 2010-03PBL (September 2010): 4.

14. Ibid.

15. Ibid.

16. Stephen G. Katsinas and Janice N. Friedel. *Uncertain Recovery: Access and Funding Issues in Public Higher Education* (Tuscaloosa, AL: University of Alabama Education Policy Center, 2010), 23–26. This covers the findings of the 2010 survey of the National Council of State Directors of Community Colleges.

17. John Pulley. "State of the States: Navigating a Difficult Road." *The Presidency Magazine* (Winter 2012): 17.

18. See http://articles.courant.com/2011-03-10/news/hc-higher-education-reorganization-0320110310_1_universities-meotti-community-colleges.

19. See www.tnr.com/article/economy/magazine/78564/austerity-economic-crisis-democrats-tea-party.

20. Gail O. Mellow and Cynthia Heelan. *Minding the Dream: The Process and Practice of the American Community College* (Lanham, MD: Rowman & Littlefield Publishers, Inc., 2008), 42–47.

21. "Pork-Barrel Report." Citizens against Government Waste, March 2, 2009. www.cagw.org/site/PageServer?pagename=reports_porkbarrelreport.

22. See http://ivytechnews.com/2011/08/29/ivy-tech-community-college-saves-over-75-million-in-3-years/.

23. Ibid.

24. See http://ivytechnews.com/2012/01/26/ivy-tech-community-college-students-save-9-5-million-on-textbooks-2/.

25. Ibid., 44.

26. See http://achievingthedream.org/about.

27. See http://thegazette.com/2012/03/13/kirkwood-village-builds-on-innovation/.

28. See http://crdnet.org/index.php?option=com_content&view=article&id=48&Itemid=46

29. Ibid., 46.

30. Ibid., 46.

31. See www.bls.gov/news.release/ecopro.nr0.htm.

32. See www.tacc.org/ecoimpact2010.htm.

COMPLETION MATTERS

1. President Barack Obama. Macomb Community College, Warren, MI, July 14, 2009.

2. *OECD Fact Book 2011–2012: Economic, Environmental and Social Statistics* (Paris, France: OECD Publishing, 2012). doi: 10.1787/factbook-2011-en.

3. "Democracy's Colleges: Call to Action." Statement made by the American Association of Community Colleges, Association of Community College Trustees, Center for Community College Student Engagement, League for Innovation in the Community College, National Institute for Staff and Organizational Development, and Phi Theta Kappa, April 2010. See http://www.accjc.org/wp-content/uploads/2010/09/Accreditation-Standards-Annotated-for-CQI-and-SLOs_Revised-June-20122.pdf .

4. According to www.ourdocuments.gov/doc.php?flash=true&doc=76, the GI Bill over seven years assisted "approximately 8 million veterans received educational benefits. Under the act, approximately 2,300,000 attended colleges and universities, 3,500,000 received school training, and 3,400,000 received on-the-job training. The number of degrees awarded by U.S. colleges and universities more than doubled between 1940 and 1950, and the percentage of Americans with bachelor degrees, or advanced degrees, rose from 4.6 percent in 1945 to 25 percent a half-century later. By 1956, when it expired, the education and training portion of the

GI Bill had disbursed $14.5 billion to veterans—but the Veterans Administration estimated the increase in federal income taxes alone would pay for the cost of the bill several times over. By 1955, 4.3 million home loans had been granted, with a total face value of $33 billion."

5. U.S. Education Secretary Arne Duncan's remarks, National Historically Black Colleges and Universities Conference, September 2, 2009.

6. Education Pays 2010. (Washington, DC: The College Board, 2010) see http://trends.collegeboard.org/downloads/Education_Pays_2010_In_Brief.pdf.

7. See www.completecollege.org/completion_shortfall/.

8. "The Heart of Student Success: Teaching, Learning, and College Completion." Center for Community College Student Engagement (Austin, TX: The University of Texas-Austin, Community College Leadership Program, 2010), p. 5.

9. William G. Bowen and Matthew M. Chingos & Michael S. McPherson. *Crossing the Finish Line: Completing College at America's Public Universities* (Princeton, NJ: Princeton University Press, 2009).

10. Ibid., 24.

11. "The Summit on Completion: Promoting the Completion Commitment." (Washington, DC: Association of Community College Trustees, 2011).

12. Ibid., 26.

13. Ibid., 27.

14. See www.all4ed.org/files/archive/publications/remediation.pdf.

15. See http://scns.fldoe.org/scns/public/pb_index.jsp.

16. See www.pasadena.edu/externalrelations/tlc/mathjam.cfm.

17. "A Matter of Degrees: Promising Practices for Community College Student Success" (Austin, TX: Center for Community College Student Engagement, 2012), 26–27.

18. Ibid., 25.

19. *2011 Community College Fast Facts* (Washington, DC: American Association of Community Colleges, 2011).

20. See www.singlestopusa.org/Strategies/Community-College.shtml.

21. See http://www.singlestopusa.org/ACCT_and_SingleStopUSA_work_together_for_student_success.pdf.

22. "Matter of Degrees," op. cit., 28.

23. See www.yorktech.com/CourseSearch/Registration_Guide.pdf, p. 5.

24. See www.whitehouse.gov/the-press-office/2010/10/05/remarks-president-and-dr-jill-biden-white-house-summit-community-college.

25. See http://chronicle.com/article/Valencia-College-Wins-First/130091/.

26. Ibid.

LEADERSHIP IMPERATIVES

1. Atul Gawande. *Better: A Surgeon's Notes on Performance* (Picado, NY: Henry Holt & Company, LLC, 2007), 246.

2. Peter D. Eckel and Matthew Harley. *Presidential Leadership in an Age of Transition: Dynamic Responses for a Turbulent Time* (Washington, DC: American Council on Education, 2011).

3. *The American College President, 2012* (Washington, DC: American Council on Education, 2012), selected statistics.

4. Richard Alfred, Christopher Shults, Ozan Janquette, and Shelley Strickland. *Challenge, Choice, or Abundance* (Lanham, MD: Rowman & Littlefield Education, in Partnership with the American Council on Education, 2009), 99–114.

5. Eckel et al., 2.

6. Alfred et al., 101.

7. *Building Communities: A Vision for a New Century.* (Washington, DC: American Association of Community and Junior Colleges, 1988), 41. This is a report of the Commission on the Future of Community Colleges.

8. Ibid.

9. The author is trying to be clever by adapting the concept of *in loco parentis*, which means "taking the place of parents," to taking the "place of the president."

10. Eckel et al., p. 2.

11. Alfred et al., p. 110.

12. See www.aacc.nche.edu/Resources/leadership/Pages/six_competencies.aspx.

13. Eckel et al., 27.

14. See www.acctsearches.org/search-guidance-for-board-of-trustees.

15. Eckel et al., 30.

16. Eckel et al., 18.

17. Eckel et al., 31.

MOVING TO THE FUTURE

1. "Coming to Our Senses: Education and the American Future." (Washington, DC: The College Board, 2008), 5. This is a report on the access, admissions, and success in higher education.

2. *Back to the Future* (Hollywood, CA: Universal Studios, 1985).

3. Claudia Goldin and Lawrence F. Katz. *The Race Between Education and Technology* (Cambridge, MA: The Belknap Press of Harvard University, 2008), 4.

4. Ibid.

5. The quotation comes from George Santayana (1863–1952), U.S. philosopher, poet. *Life of Reason: Reason in Common Sense* (New York: C. Scribner's Sons, 1905–1906), chapter 12.

6. See the American Servicemen's Readjustment Act at www.ourdocuments.gov/doc.php?flash=true&doc=76.

7. "Veterans Enrolled in Higher Education under GI Bills, as percentage of total enrollment: 1947–1997" (Washington, DC: Historical Statistics of the United States, 2006).

8. Milton Greenberg. *The GI Bill of Rights—Historians on America: Decisions That Made a Difference* (Washington, DC: U.S. Department of State, Bureau of International Information Programs, 2010), 50.

9. See www.economics-charts.com/gdp/gdp-1929-2004.html.

10. See www.bea.gov/newsreleases/national/gdp/gdpnewsrelease.htm.

11. To approximate what the conversion of 1944 dollars would be to 2011 dollars, I used the U.S. Department of Labor's Bureau of Labor Statistics conversion module at http://data.bls.gov/cgi-bin/cpicalc.pl.

12. See http://costofwar.com/en/publications/2011/annual-costs-war-afghanistan/.

13. Supplemental Appropriations Act of 2008 (Public Law 110-252, H.R. 2642), signed into law on June 30, 2008.

14. See http://www.monticello.org/site/jefferson/quotations-education.

15. "Higher Education for Democracy: A Report of the President's Commission on Higher Education," Volume 1, Establishing the Goals (Washington, DC: U.S. Government Printing Office, 1947), 1.

16. See www.ida.org/upload/stpi/pdfs/ida-d-3306.pdf, p. vii–1.

17. President John F. Kennedy. Speech to Special Joint Session of Congress on May 25, 1961.

18. See http://lawhighereducation.com/75-higher-education-act-hea.html.

19. See www2.ed.gov/about/reports/annual/2011report/fsa-report.pdf.

20. Thomas L. Friedman. *The World is Flat: A Brief History of the Twenty-First Century* (New York: Farrar, Straus and Giroux, 2005), 290.

21. Charles Caleb Colton (1780–1832) was a British author, clergyman, and art collector, who is credited for the phrase "imitation is the sincerest form of flattery."

22. David Pluviose. "Why Is Alan Greenspan Talking Up Community Colleges?" *Community College Week*, August 22, 2005.

23.   See http://online.wsj.com/article/SB10001424052748703431604575521711498542310
.html.

24.   Excerpted from the State of the Union Address, delivered by President George W.
Bush, January 20, 2004.

25.   See www.doleta.gov/TAACCCT/.

26.   *Building Communities: A Vision for a New Century.* (Washington, DC: American
Association of Community and Junior Colleges, 1988), 45. This is a report made by the
Commission of the Future of Community Colleges.

27.   *The Knowledge Net: Connecting Communities, Learners, and Colleges* (Washington,
DC: America Association of Community Colleges, 2000), 31.

28.   *Winning the Skills Race and Strengthening America's Middle Class: An Action Agenda
for Community Colleges* (New York: The College Board, 2008), 33.

29.   See www.consumerfinance.gov/blog/too-big-to-fail-student-debt-hits-a-trillion/.

30.   See www.aacc.nche.edu/Advocacy/toolkit/Documents/memo_oped.pdf.

31.   President William Jefferson Clinton. Presidential Inaugural Address to the Nation,
January 20, 1993.

Index

About the Author

J. Noah Brown is the fourth president and chief executive officer of the Association of Community College Trustees (ACCT). An experienced association executive specializing in public policy, legislative advocacy, and strategic planning, Noah is a nationally recognized authority on community college governance, a contributor to national publications, and a speaker on a broad range of topics to large audiences. Noah provides national leadership on behalf of more than 6,000 elected and appointed officials governing 1,200 community colleges throughout the United States. Much of his work has focused on strengthening the strategic connections between community college boards and the array of national and state organizations important to supporting the mission of community colleges. Married with two daughters, Noah resides in Bethesda, Maryland, along with the family pug Ginger.